FOR ORGANS, PIANOS & ELECTRONIC KEYBOARDS

E-Z PLAY TODAY

180

ISBN 978-1-4950-3510-4

HAL•LEONARD®
CORPORATION
7777 W. BLUEMOUND RD. P.O. BOX 13819 MILWAUKEE, WI 53213

In Australia Contact:
Hal Leonard Australia Pty. Ltd.
4 Lentara Court
Cheltenham, Victoria, 3192 Australia
Email: ausadmin@halleonard.com.au

Visit Hal Leonard Online at
www.halleonard.com

Alleluia
from EXSULTATE, JUBILATE

Registration 1
Rhythm: None

By Wolfgang Amadeus Mozart

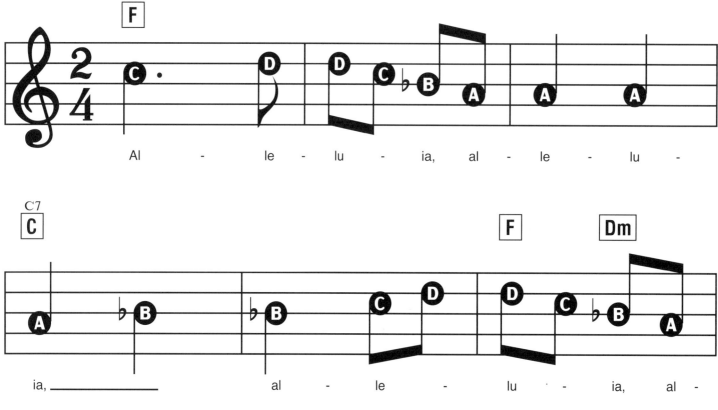

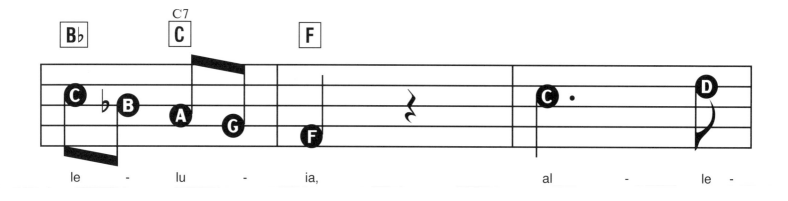

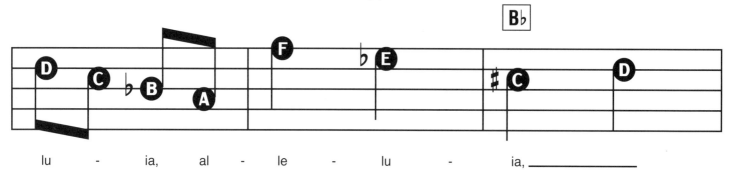

3

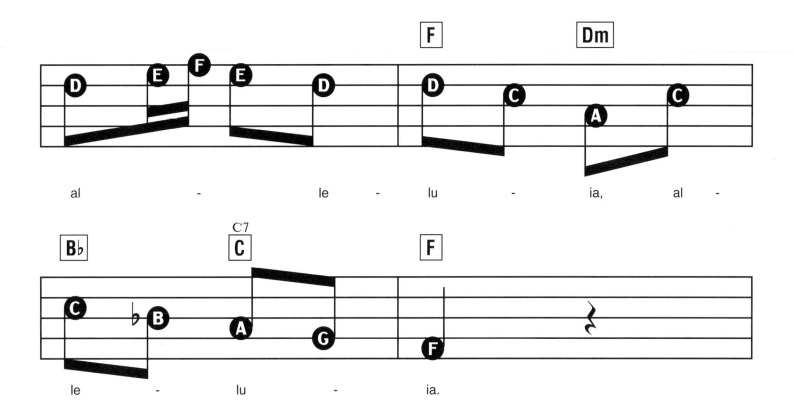

al - le - lu - ia, al -

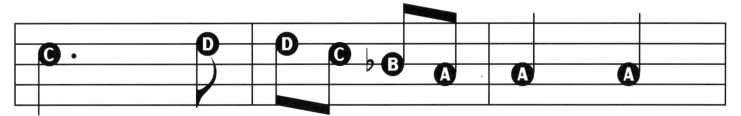

le - lu - ia.

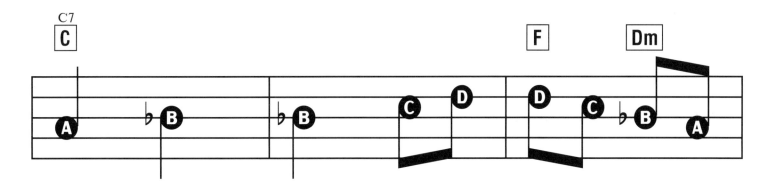

(Instrumental)

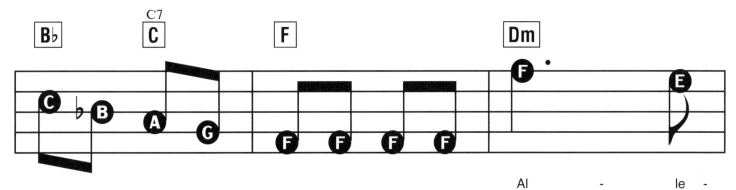

Al - le -

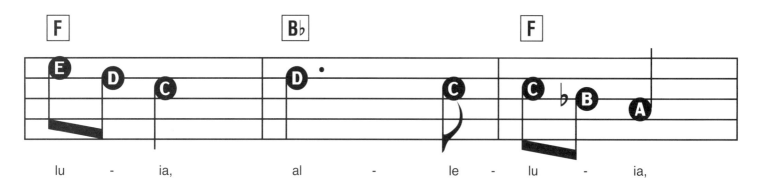

lu - ia, al - le - lu - ia,

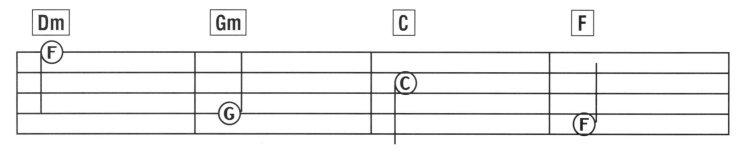

al - le - lu - ia,

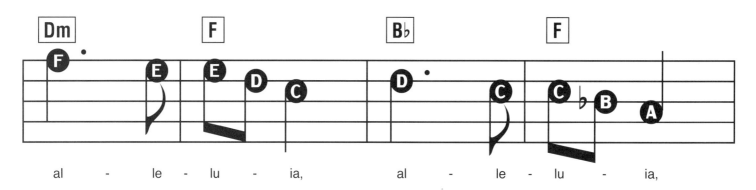

al - le - lu - ia, al - le - lu - ia,

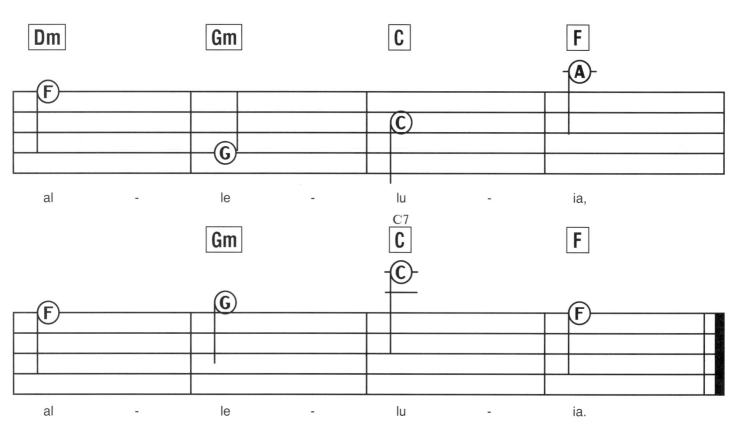

al - le - lu - ia,

al - le - lu - ia.

Ave verum corpus
K. 618

Registration 6
Rhythm: Ballad or None

By Wolfgang Amadeus Mozart

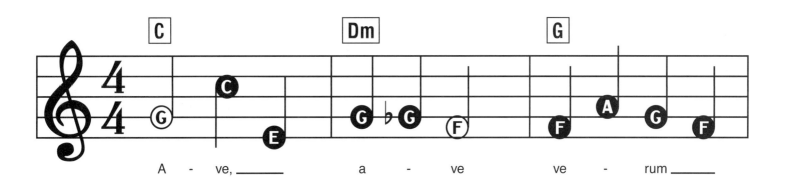

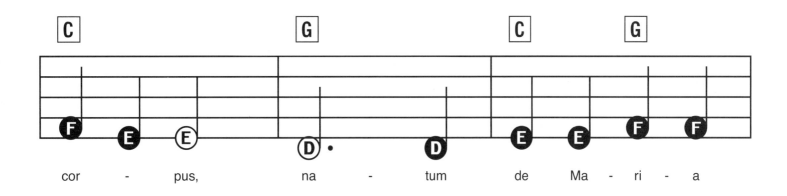

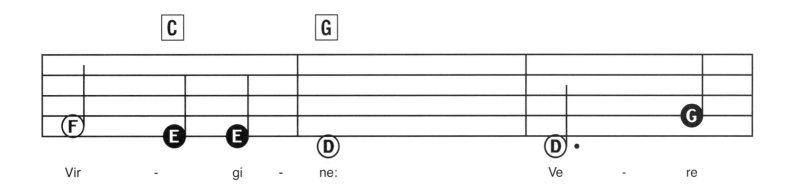

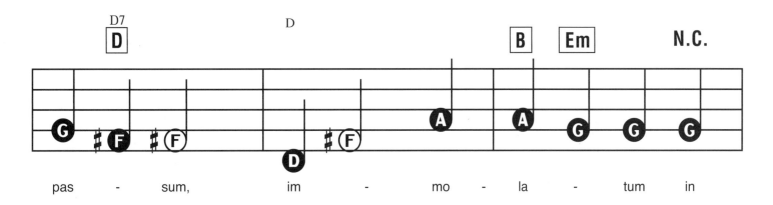

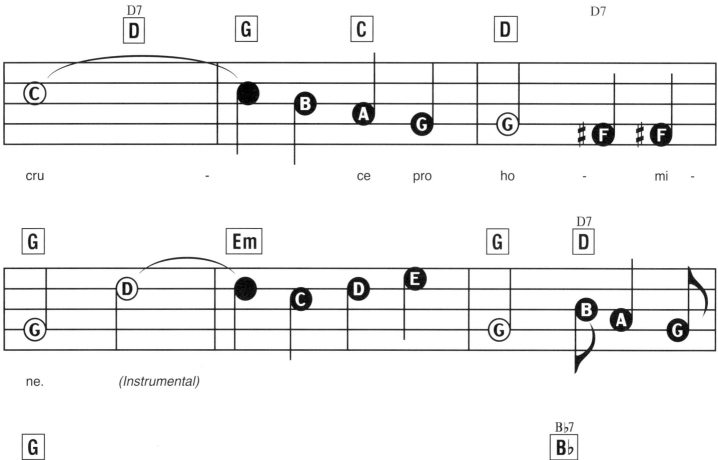

cru - - - ce pro ho - mi -

ne. *(Instrumental)*

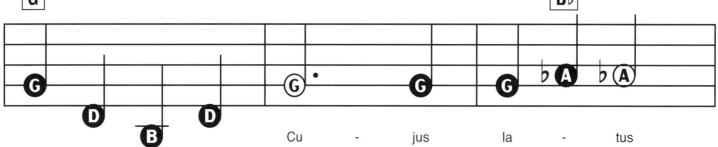

Cu - jus la - tus

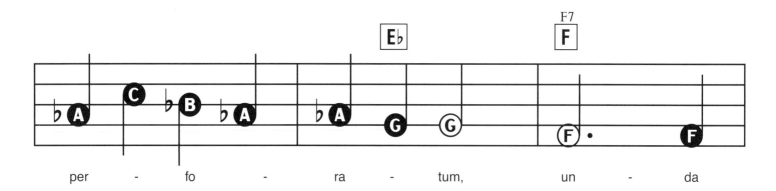

per - fo - ra - tum, un - da

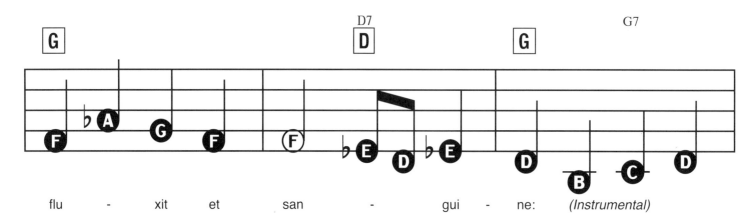

flu - xit et san - gui - ne: *(Instrumental)*

7

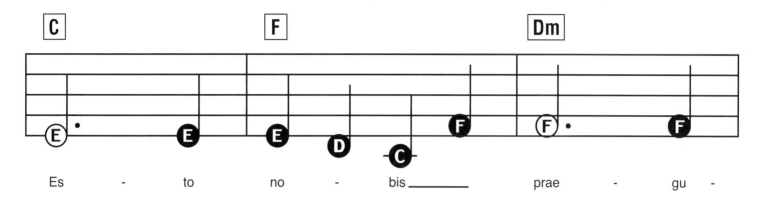

Es - to no - bis _____ prae - gu -

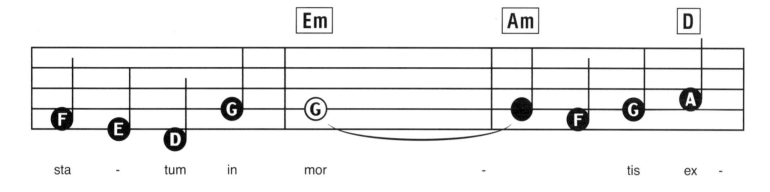

sta - tum in mor - tis ex -

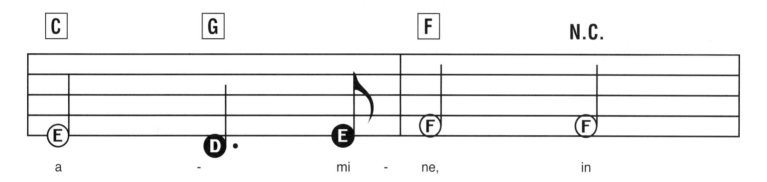

a - mi - ne, in

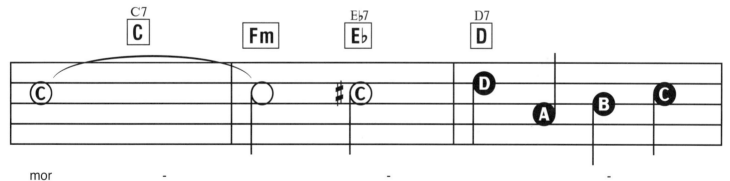

mor - - -

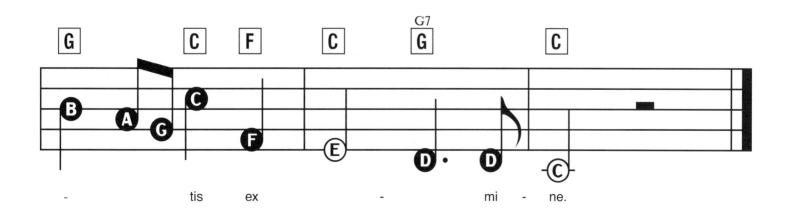

- tis ex - mi - ne.

Concerto for Clarinet in A Major
Second Movement

Registration 1
Rhythm: None

By Wolfgang Amadeus Mozart

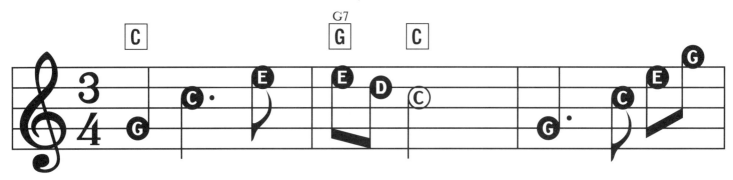

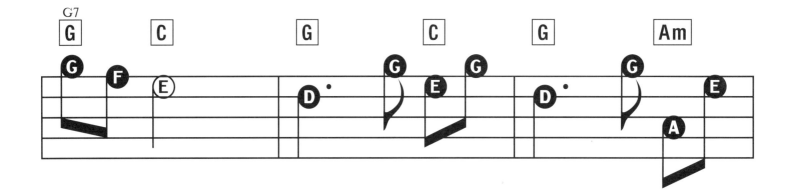

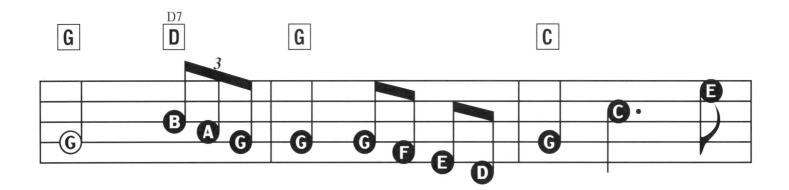

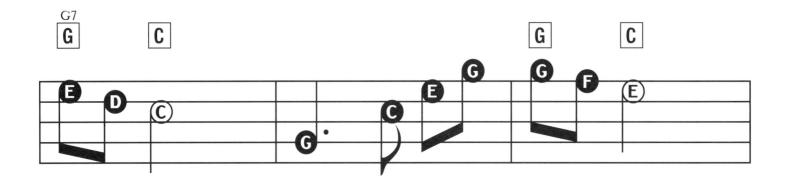

9

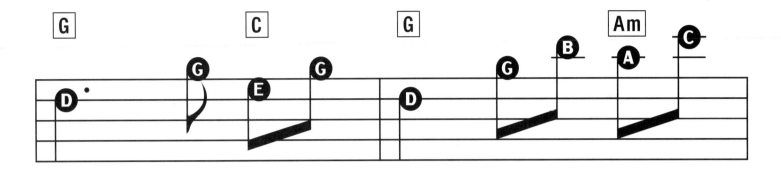

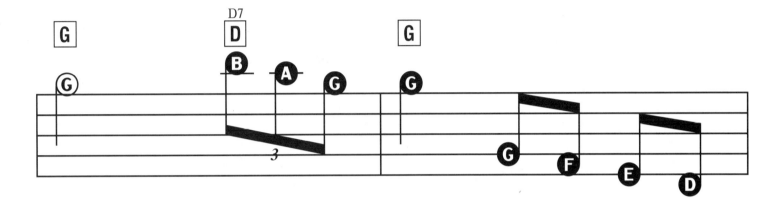

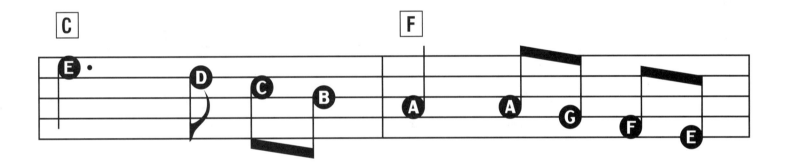

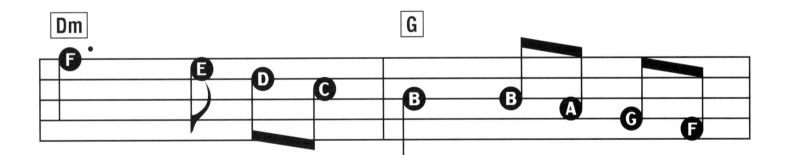

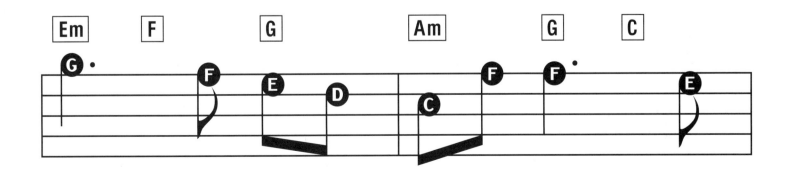

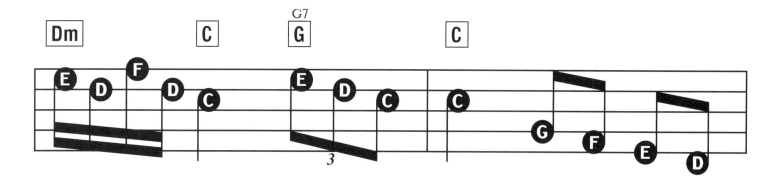

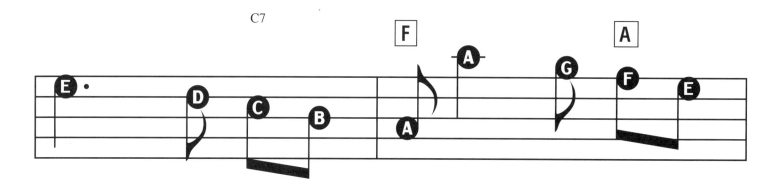

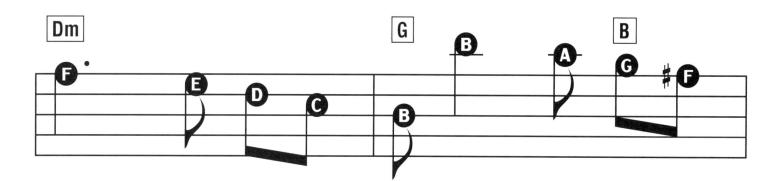

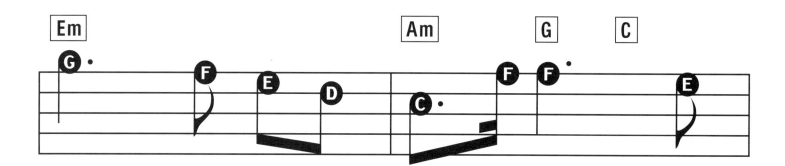

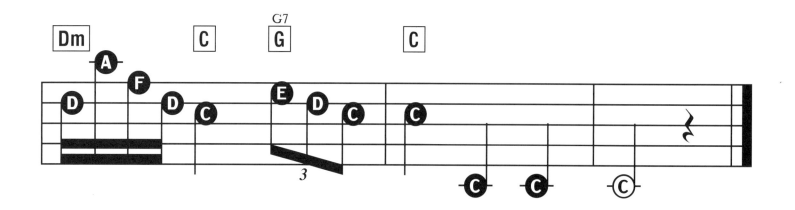

Eine kleine Nachtmusik
Second Movement (Romanze)

Registration 3
Rhythm: Ballad or None

By Wolfgang Amadeus Mozart

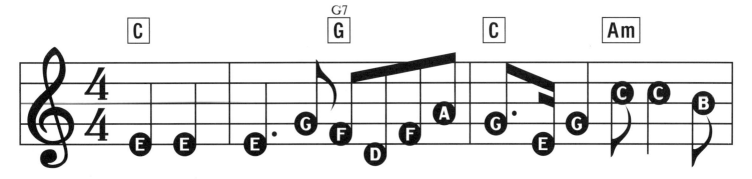

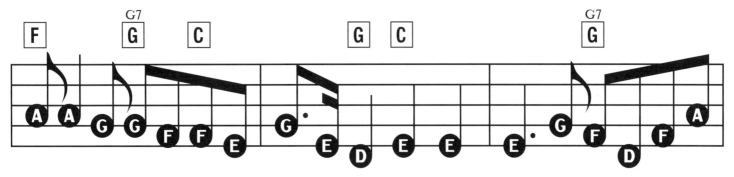

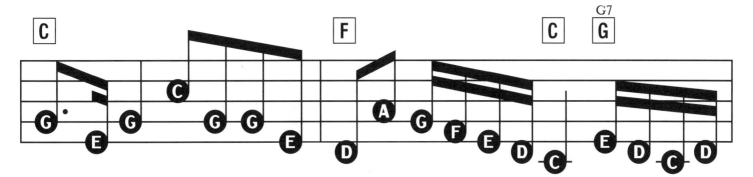

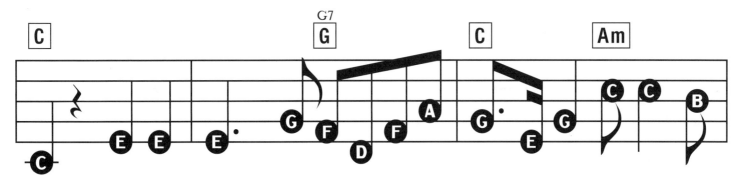

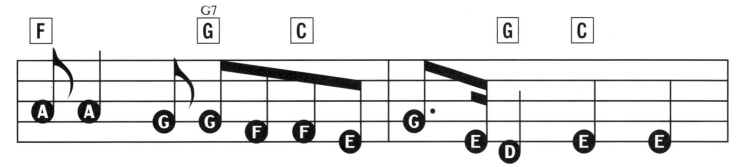

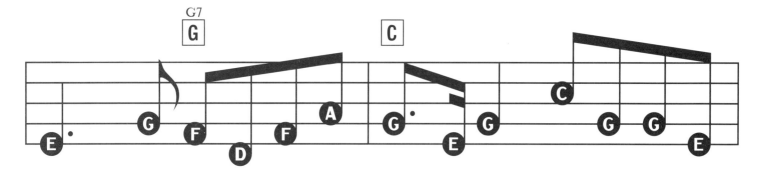

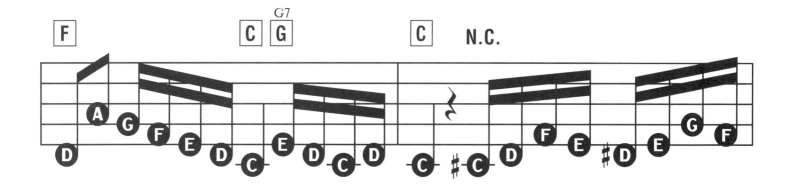

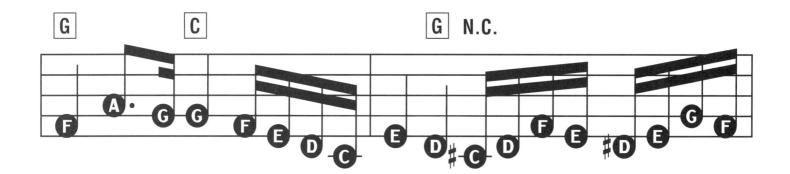

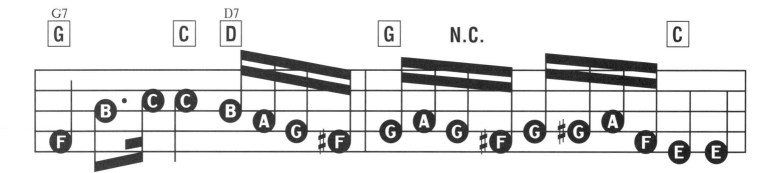

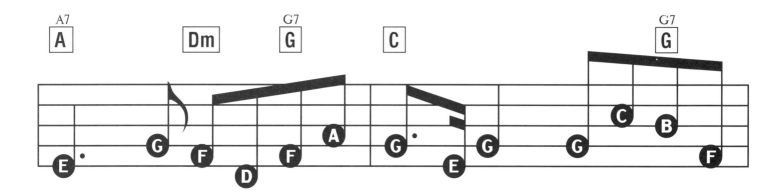

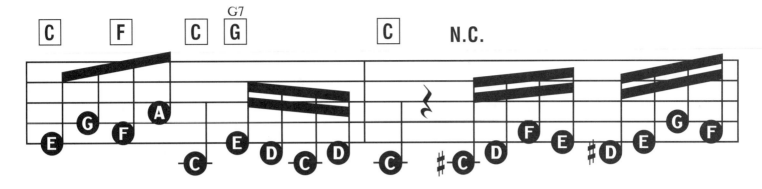

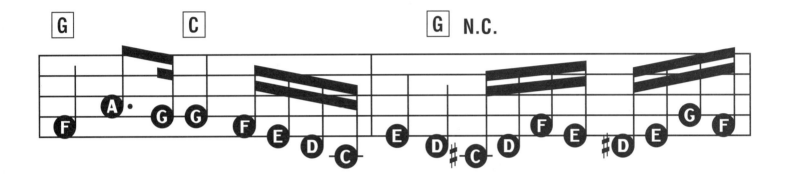

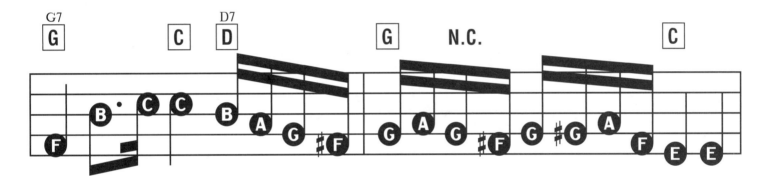

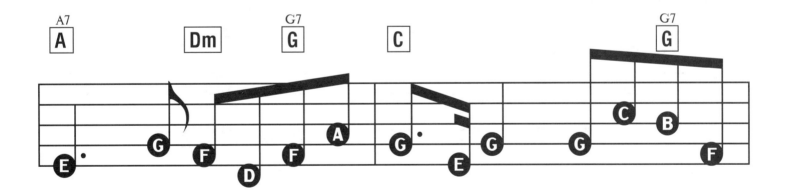

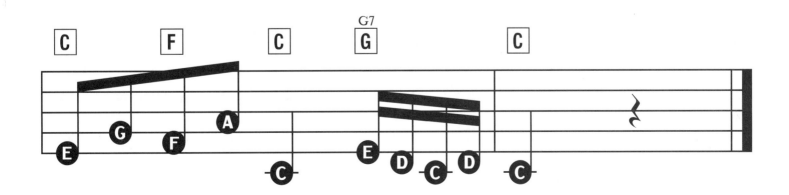

Contessa, perdono
from LE NOZZE DI FIGARO

Registration 1
Rhythm: Ballad

By Wolfgang Amadeus Mozart

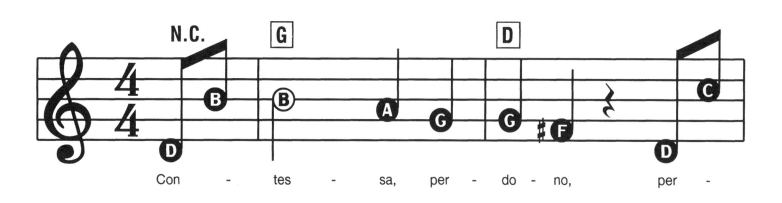

Con - tes - sa, per - do - no, per -

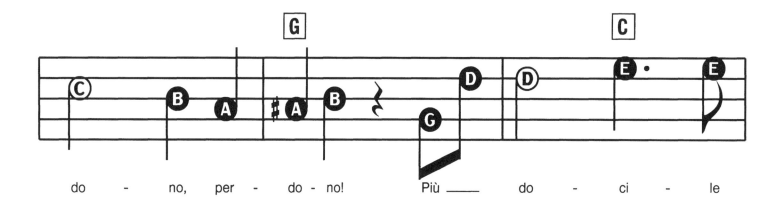

do - no, per - do - no! Più ____ do - ci - le

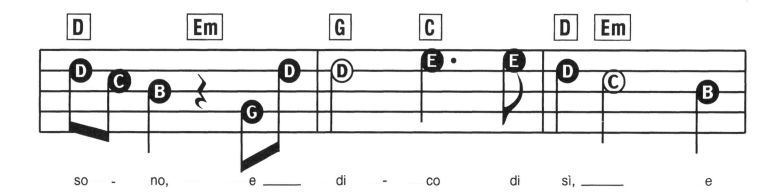

so - no, e ____ di - co di sì, ____ e

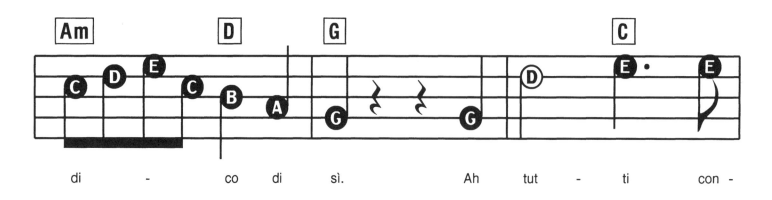

di - co di sì. Ah tut - ti con -

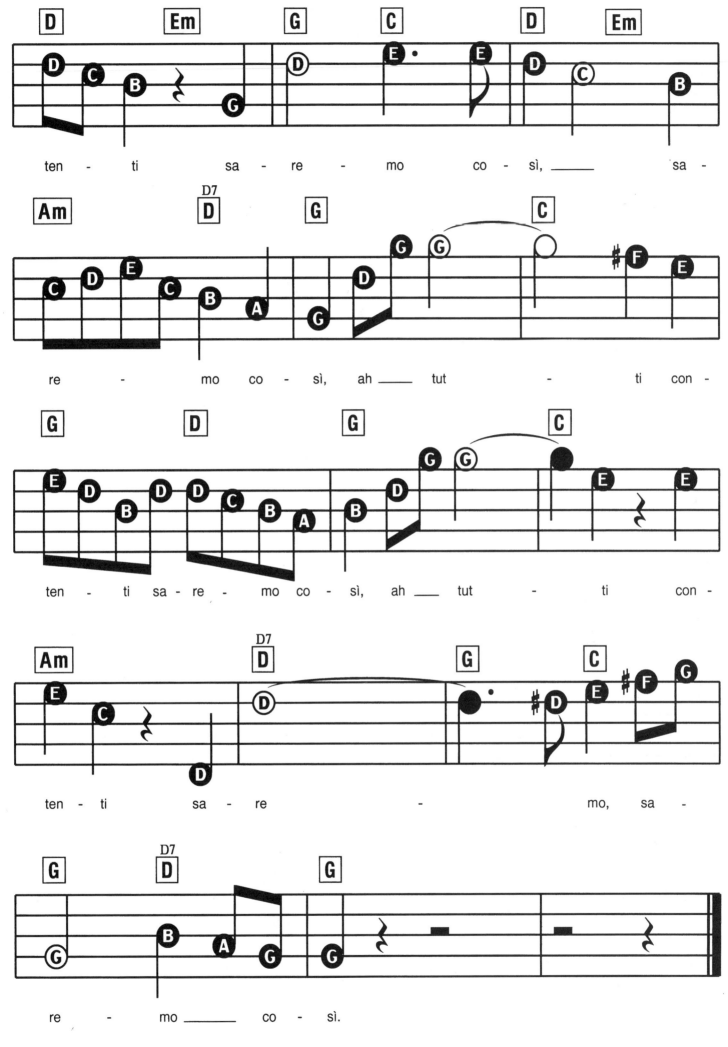

Deh, vieni alla finestra
(Serenade)
from DON GIOVANNI

Registration 3
Rhythm: Waltz

By Wolfgang Amadeus Mozart

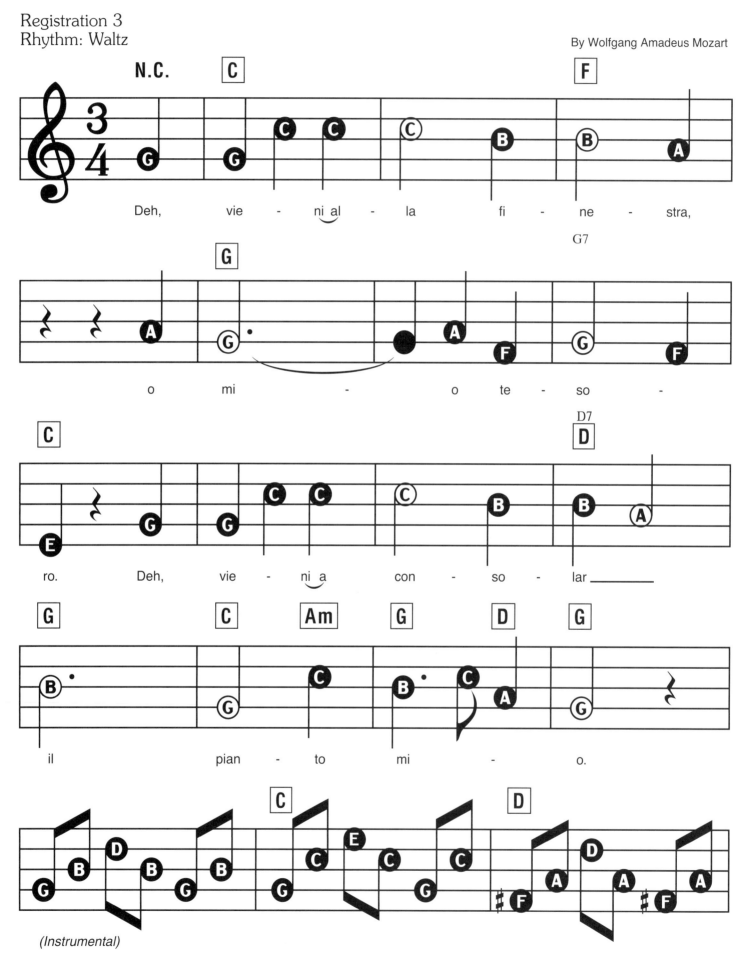

(Instrumental)

17

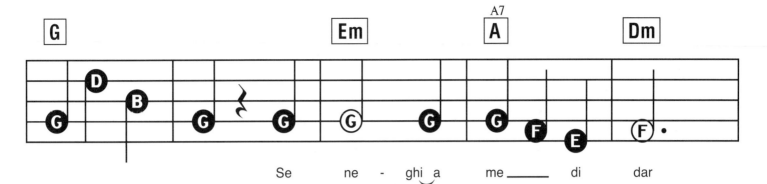

Se ne - ghi a me _____ di dar

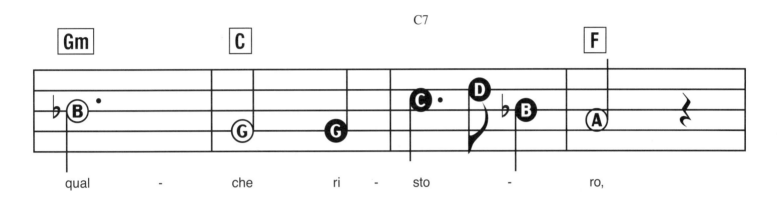

qual - che ri - sto - ro,

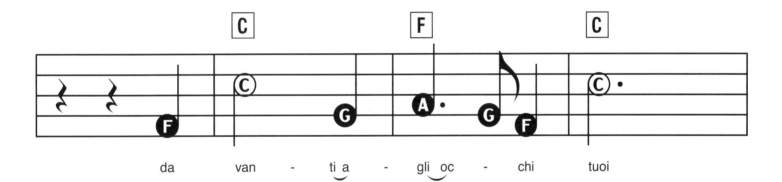

da van - ti a - gli oc - chi tuoi

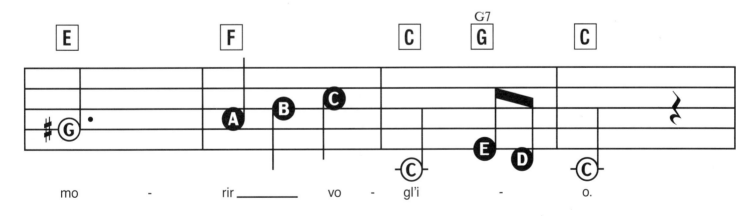

mo - rir _____ vo - gl'i - o.

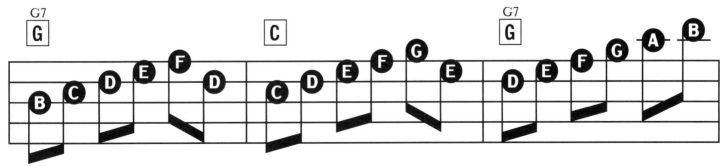

(Instrumental)

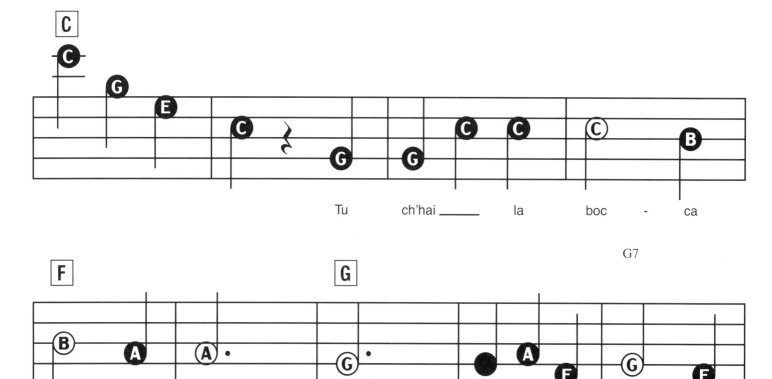

Tu ch'hai _____ la boc - ca

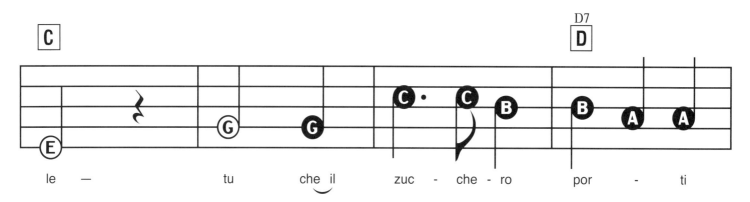

dol - ce più _____ che il mie -

le — tu che il zuc - che - ro por - ti

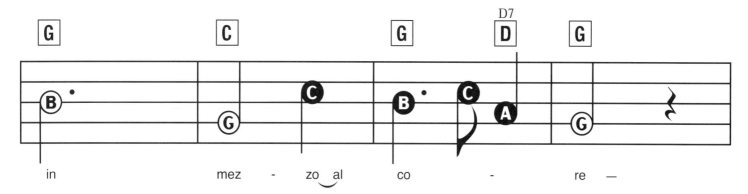

in mez - zo al co - re —

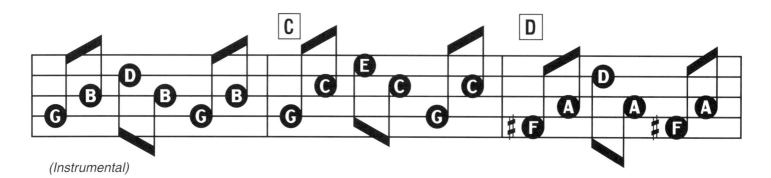

(Instrumental)

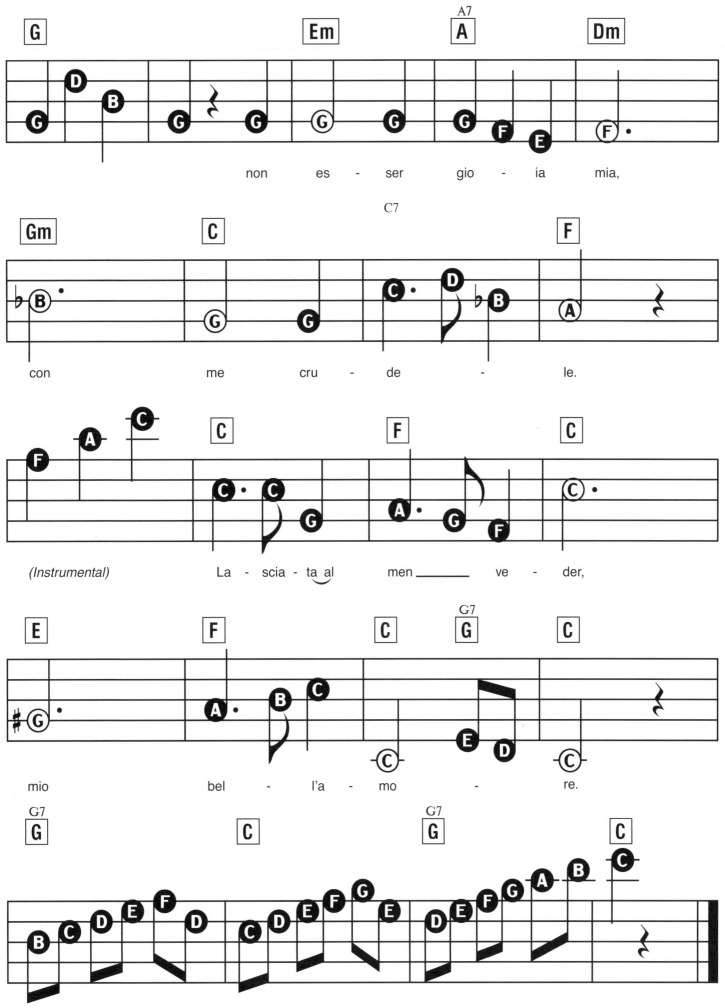

non es - ser gio - ia mia,

con me cru - de - le.

(Instrumental) La - scia - ta al men _____ ve - der,

mio bel - l'a - mo - re.

(Instrumental)

Der Hölle Rache
from THE MAGIC FLUTE

Registration 7
Rhythm: March

By Wolfgang Amadeus Mozart

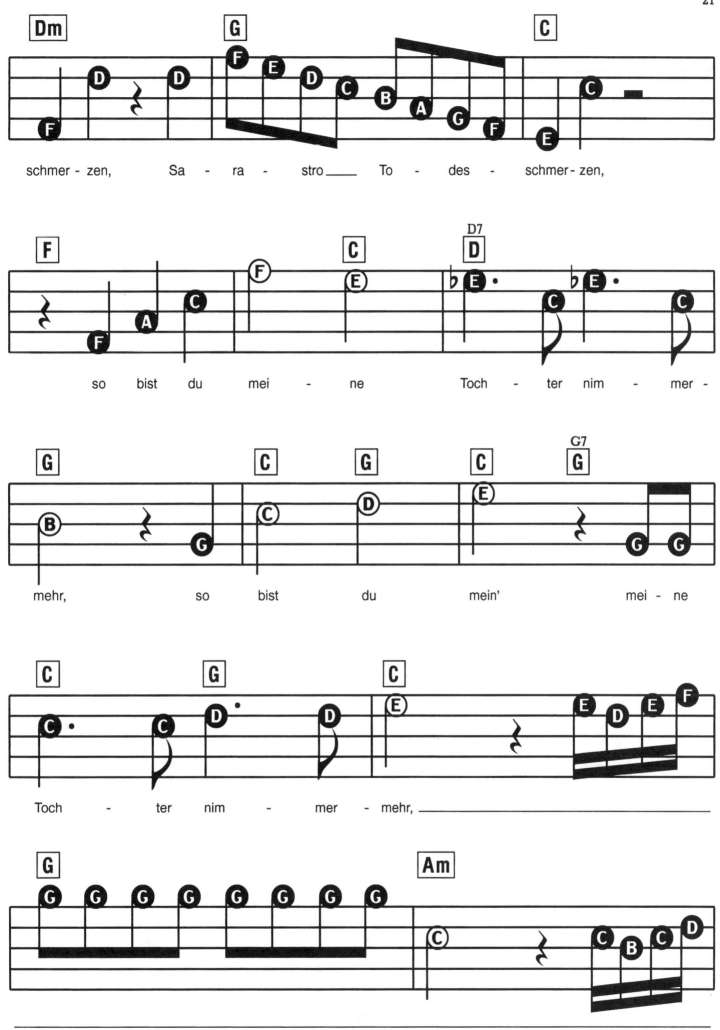

22

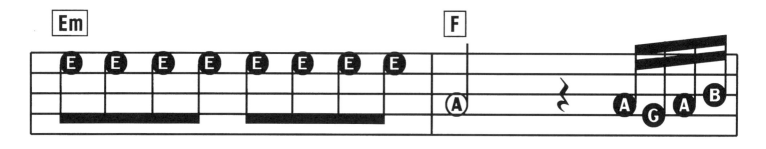

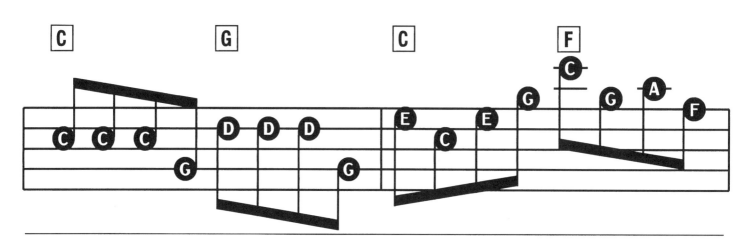

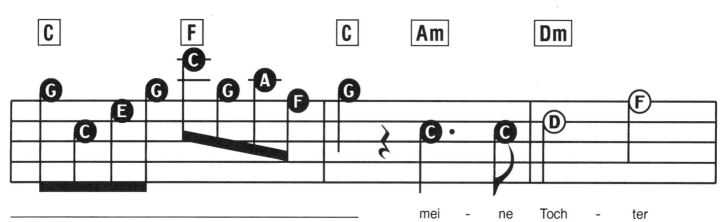

mei - ne Toch - ter

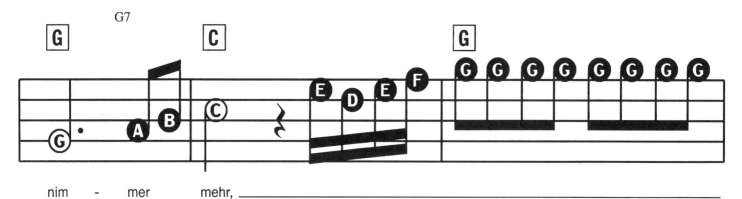

nim - mer mehr,

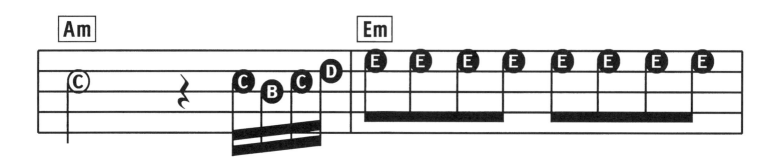

23

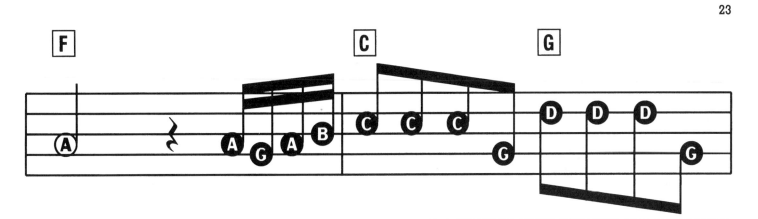

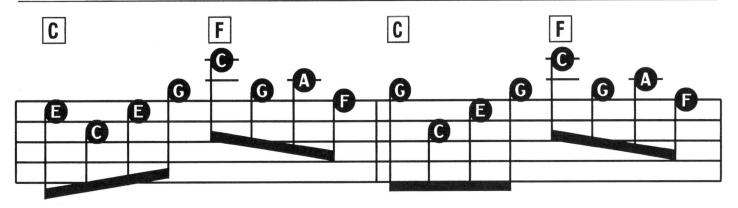

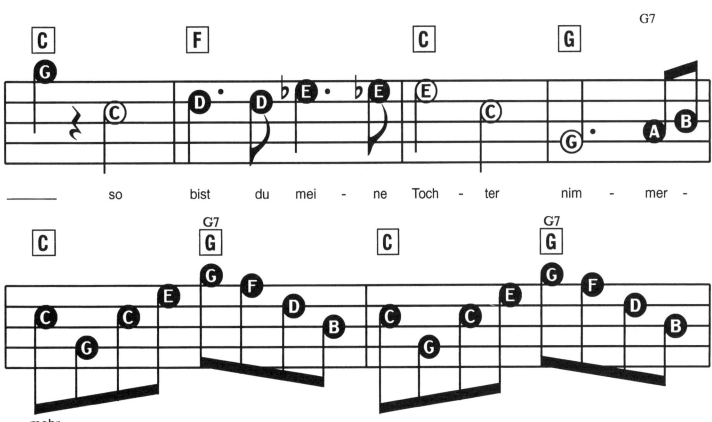

so bist du mei - ne Toch - ter nim - mer -

mehr.

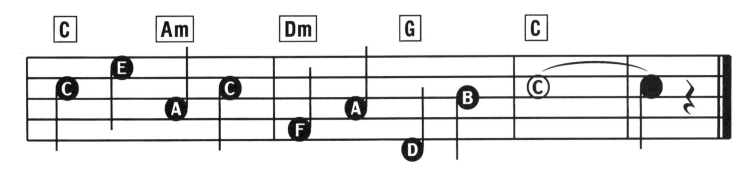

Der Vogelfänger bin ich ja
from THE MAGIC FLUTE

Registration 5
Rhythm: March or Fox Trot

Words by Emanuel Schikaneder
Music by Wolfgang Amadeus Mozart

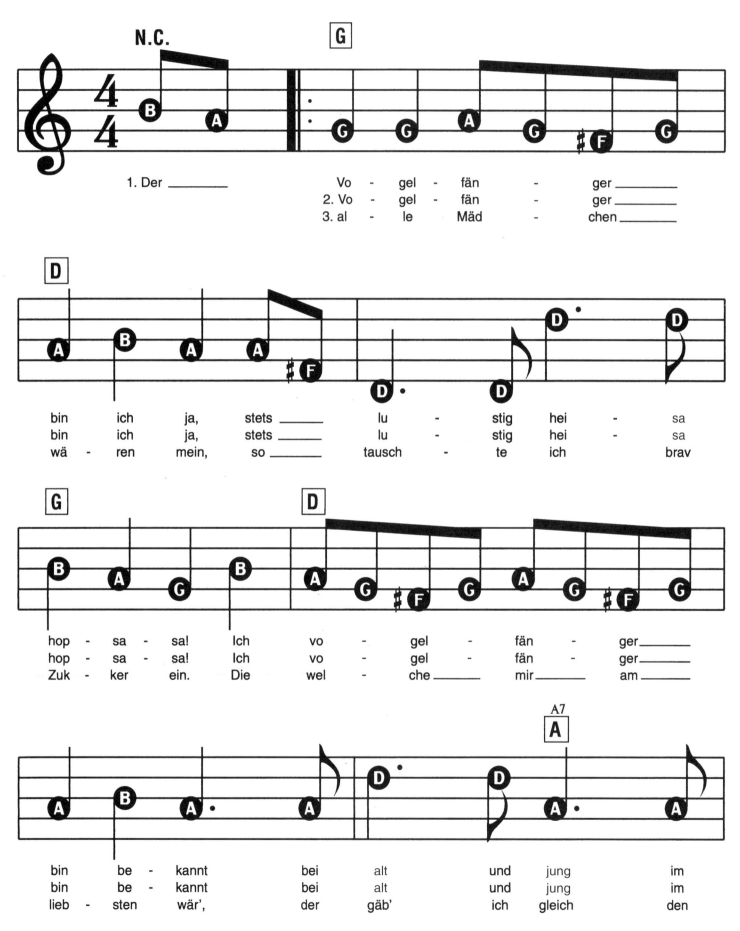

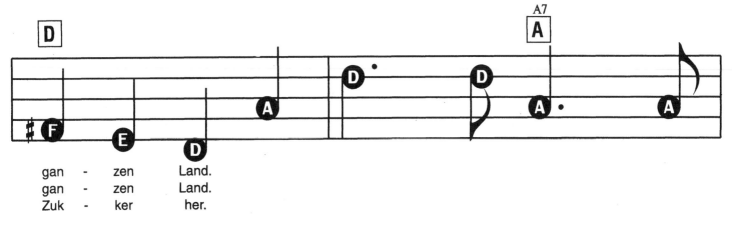

gan - zen Land.
gan - zen Land.
Zuk - ker her.

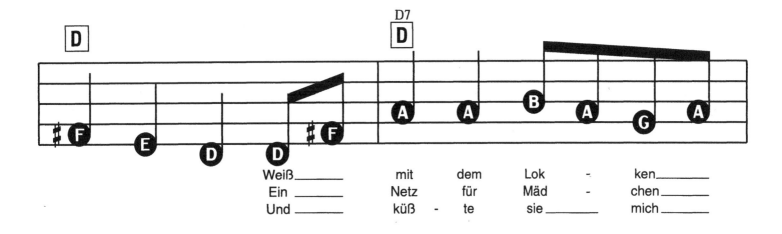

Weiß_____ mit dem Lok - ken_____
Ein _____ Netz für Mäd - chen_____
Und _____ küß - te sie _____ mich _____

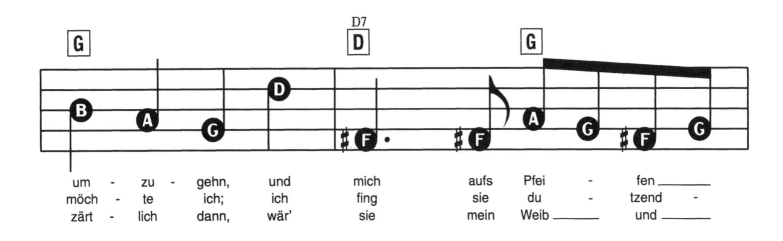

um - zu - gehn, und mich aufs Pfei - fen _____
möch - te ich; und ich mich fing sie du - tzend -
zärt - lich dann, wär' sie mein Weib _____ und _____

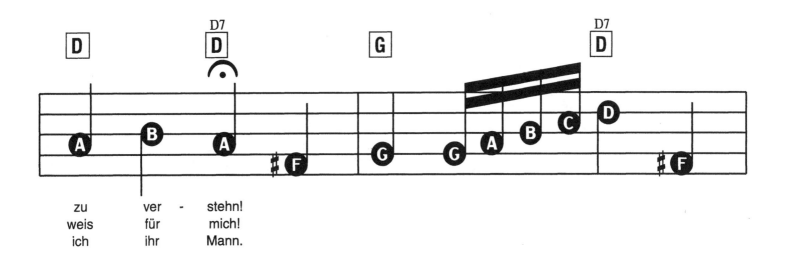

zu ver - stehn!
weis für mich!
ich ihr Mann.

Drum _____ kann ich froh _____ und _____
Dann _____ sperr - te ich _____ sie _____
Sie _____ schleif an mei - ner _____

lu - stig sein, denn _____ al - le Vö - gel _____
bei mir ein, und _____ al - le Mäd - chen _____
Sei - te ein; ich _____ wieg - te wie _____ ein _____

sind ja _____ mein.
wä - ren _____ mein.
Kind sie _____ ein.

2. Der _____
3. Wenn _____

Là ci darem la mano
from DON GIOVANNI

Registration 1
Rhythm: Ballad

By Wolfgang Amadeus Mozart

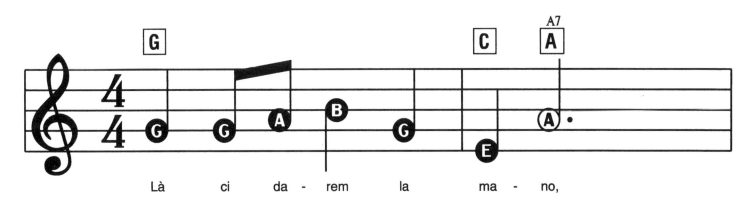

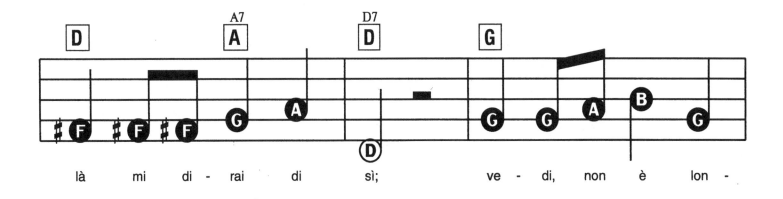

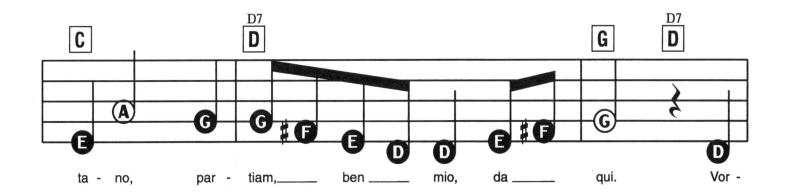

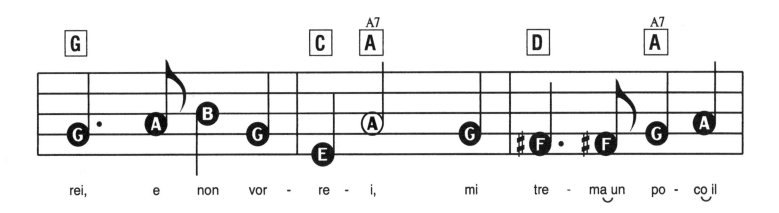

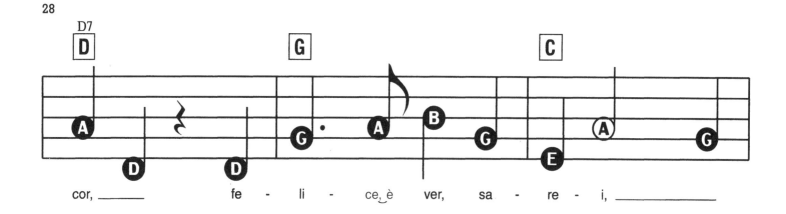

cor, _____ fe - li - ce̱ è ver, sa - re - i, _____

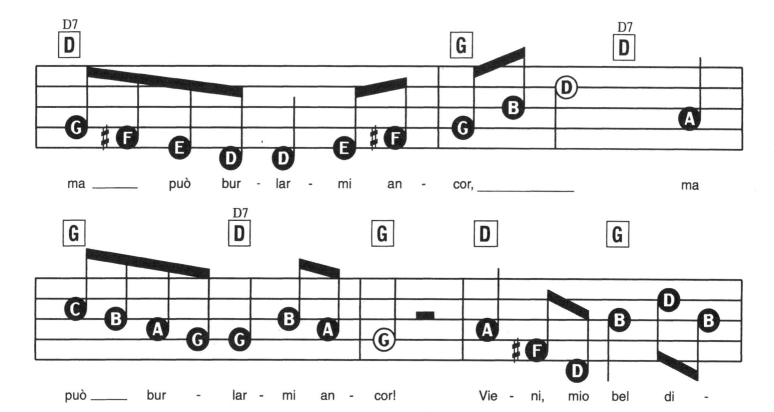

ma _____ può bur - lar - mi an - cor, _____ ma

può _____ bur - lar - mi an - cor! Vie - ni, mio bel di -

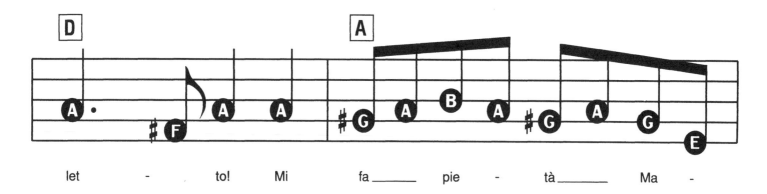

let - to! Mi fa_____ pie - tà_____ Ma -

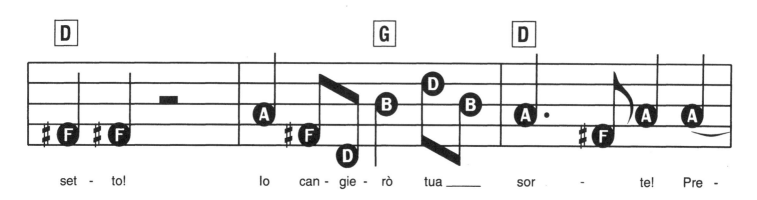

set - to! Io can - gie - rò tua _____ sor - te! Pre -

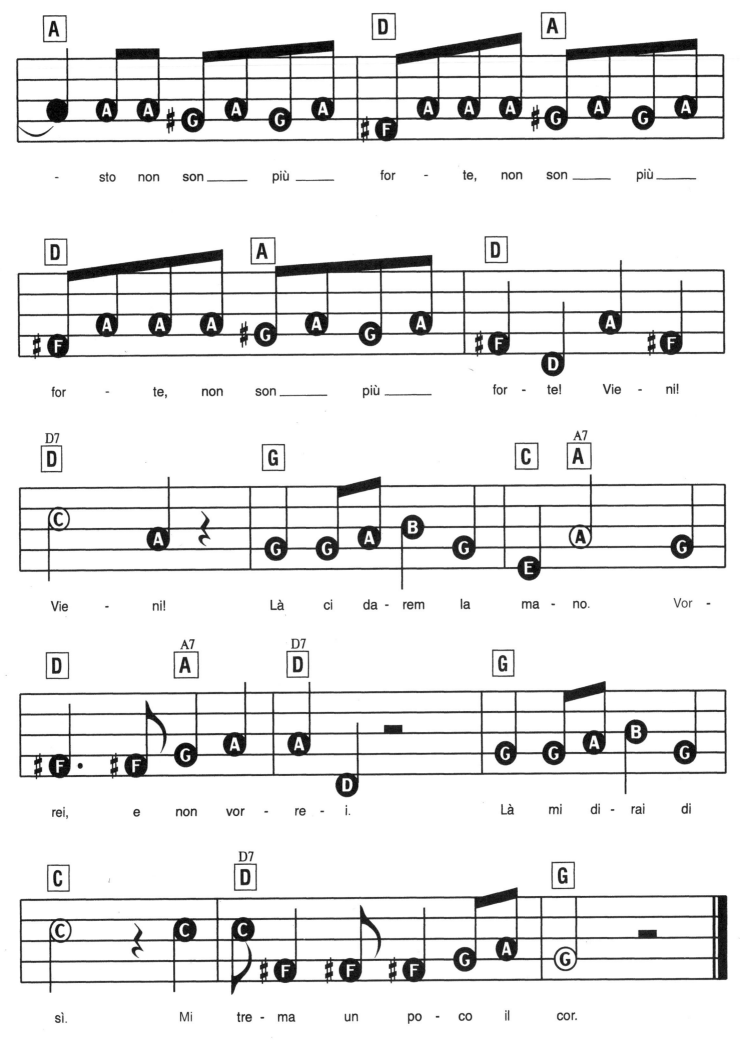

Eine kleine Nachtmusik
First Movement (Allegro)

Registration 3
Rhythm: None

By Wolfgang Amadeus Mozart

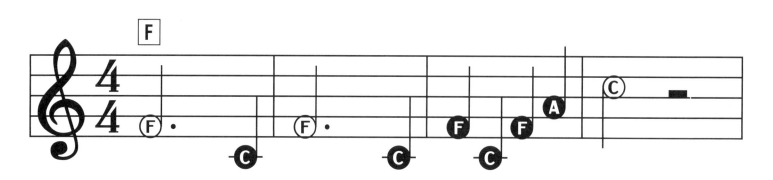

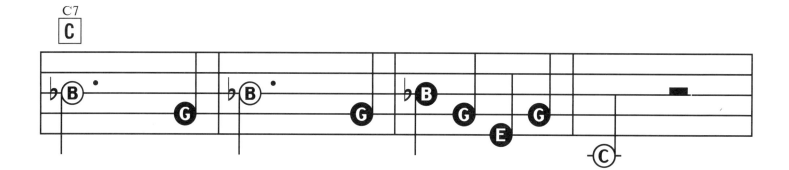

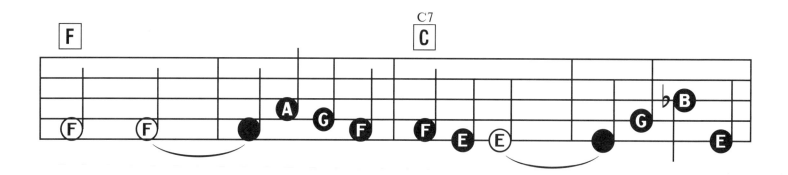

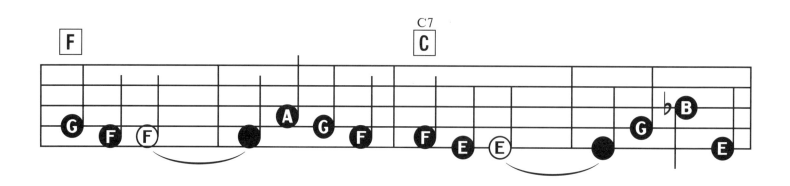

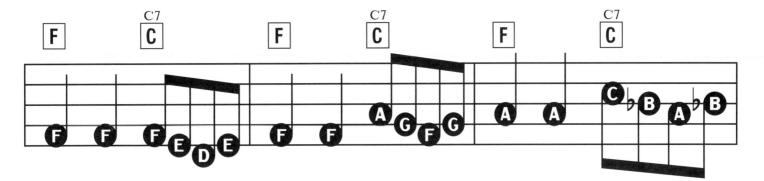

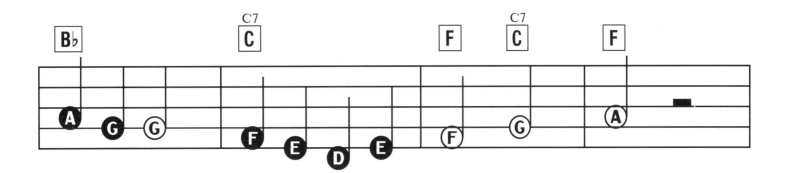

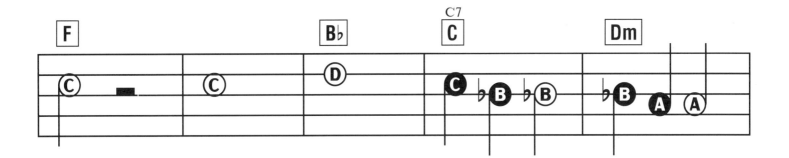

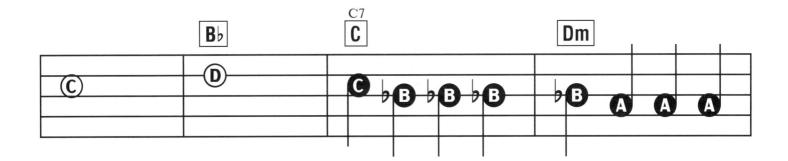

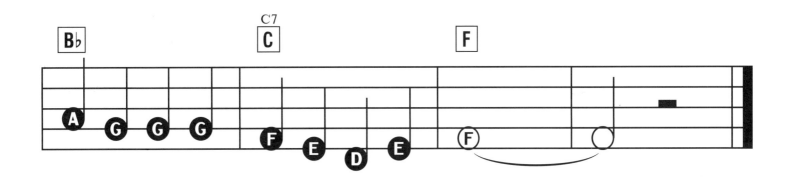

31

Eine kleine Nachtmusik
Third Movement (Menuetto)

Registration 3
Rhythm: Waltz or None

By Wolfgang Amadeus Mozart

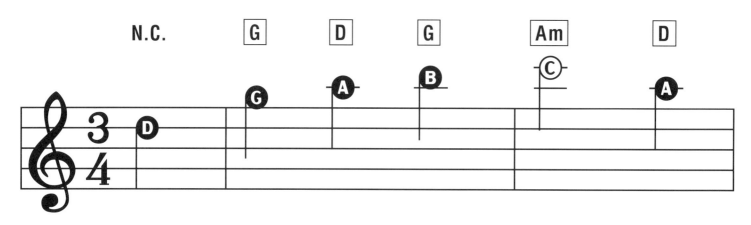

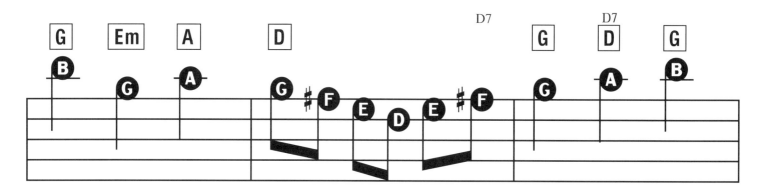

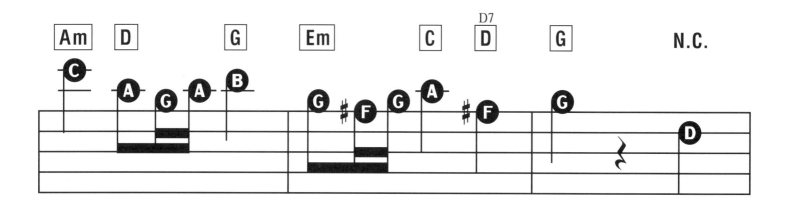

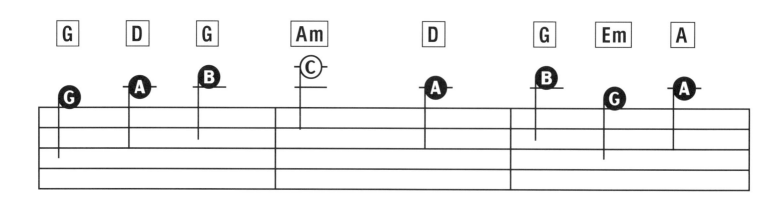

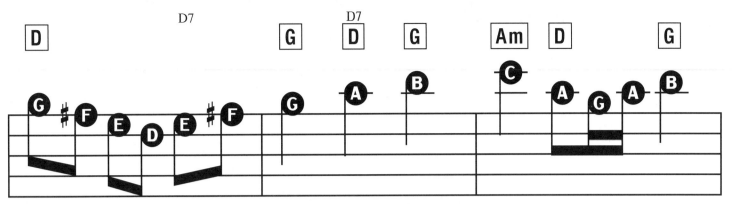

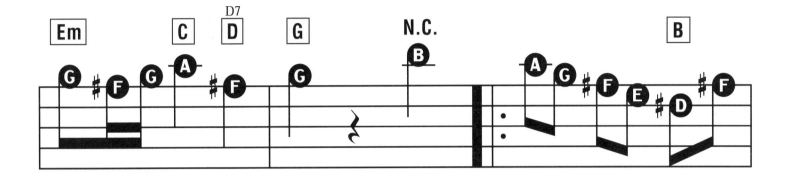

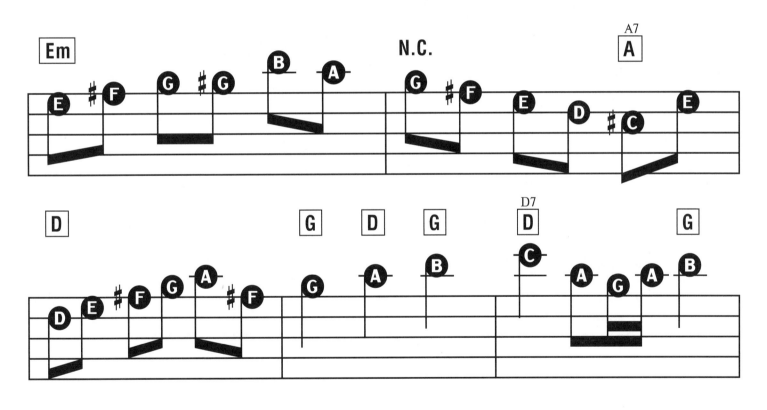

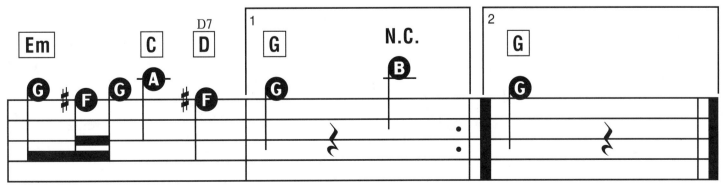

Eine kleine Nachtmusik
Fourth Movement (Rondo)

Registration 3
Rhythm: March or Polka

By Wolfgang Amadeus Mozart

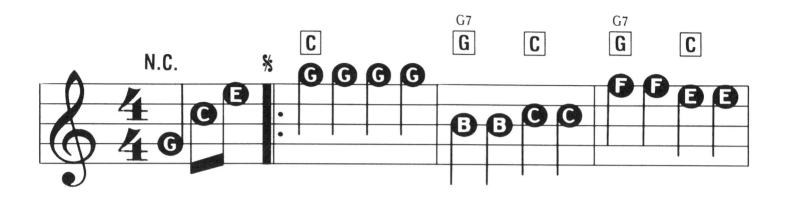

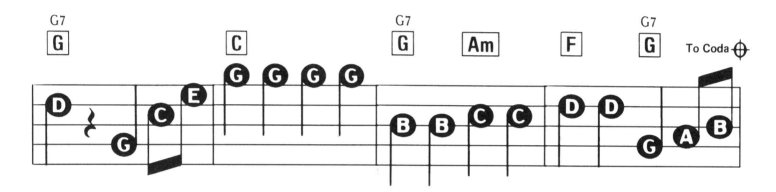

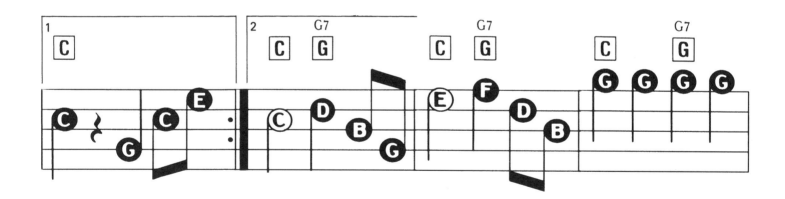

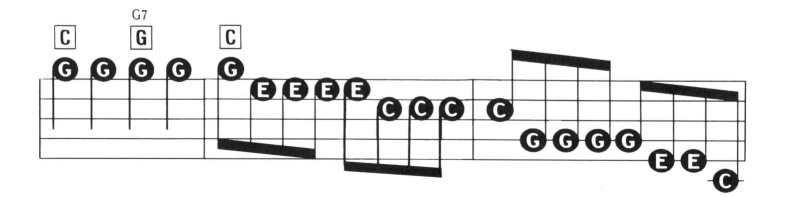

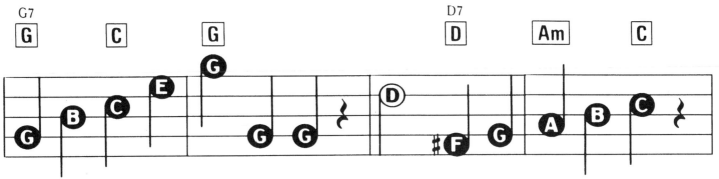

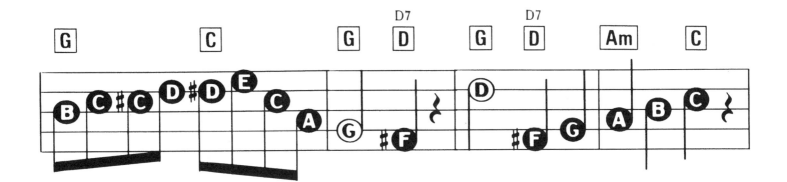

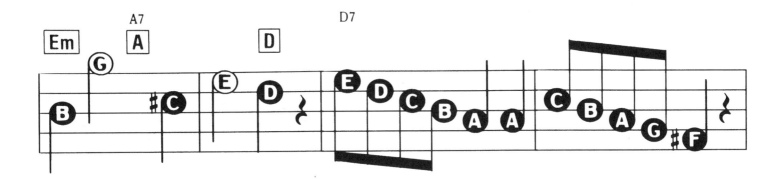

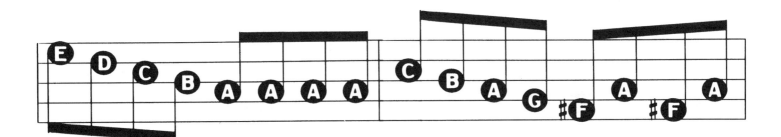

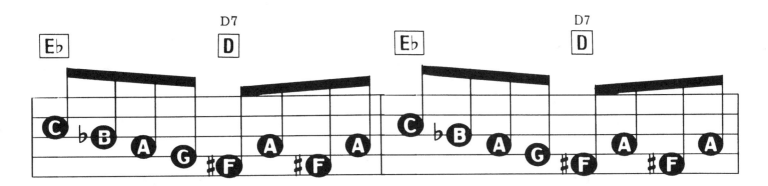

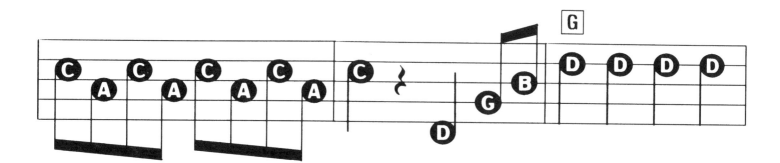

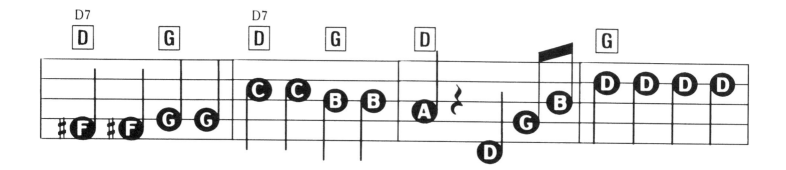

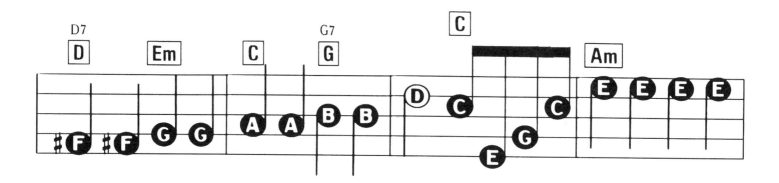

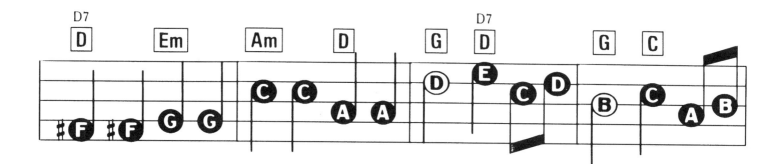

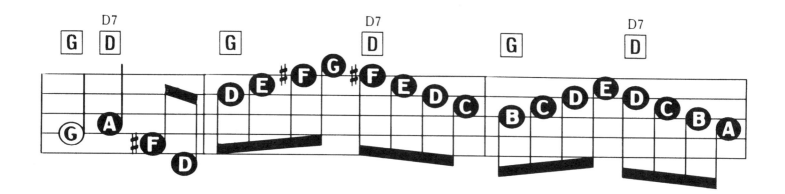

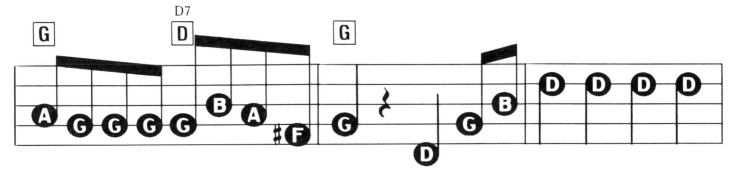

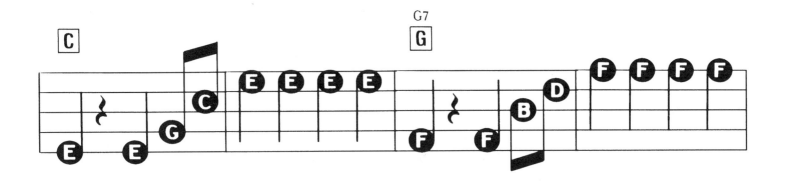

D.S. al Coda
(Return to %
Play to ⊕ and
skip to Coda)

⊕ **CODA**

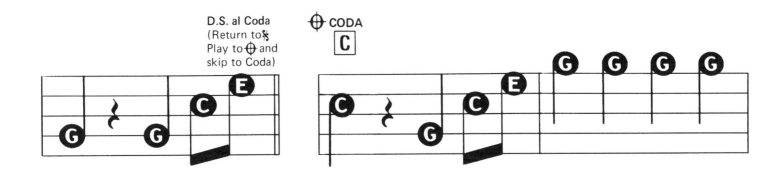

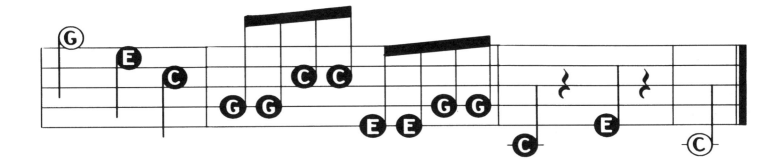

German Dance in C Major
K. 605, No. 3

Registration 2
Rhythm: Waltz or None

By Wolfgang Amadeus Mozart

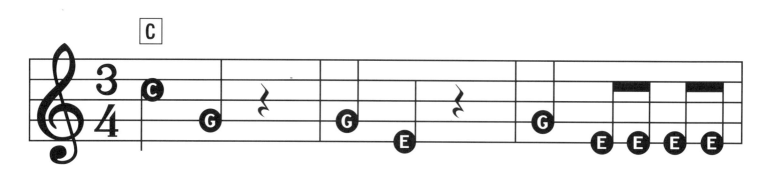

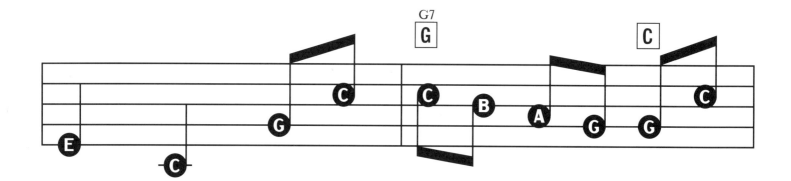

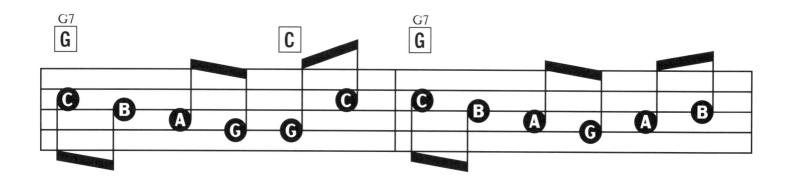

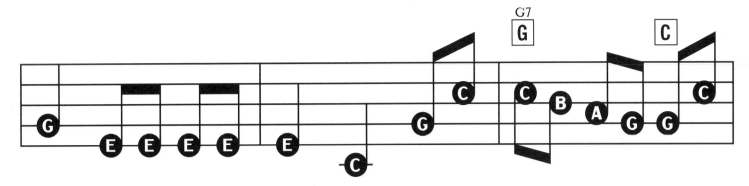
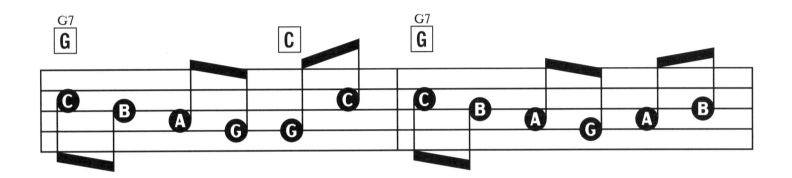
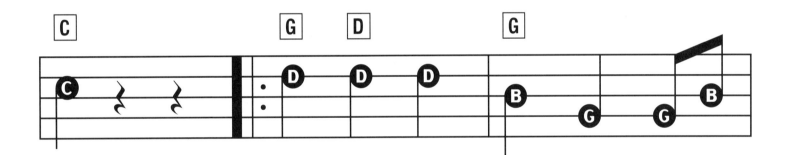
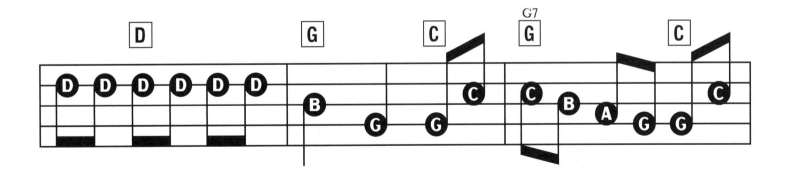
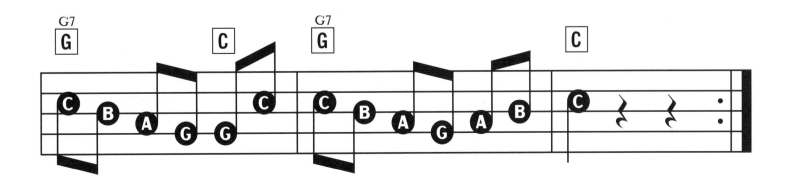

Minuet
from DON GIOVANNI

Registration 3
Rhythm: Waltz

By Wolfgang Amadeus Mozart

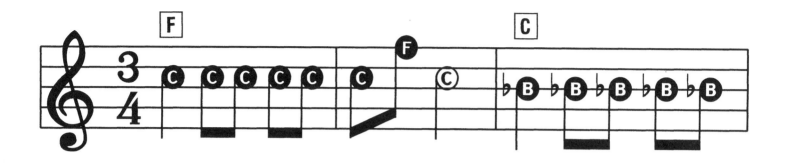

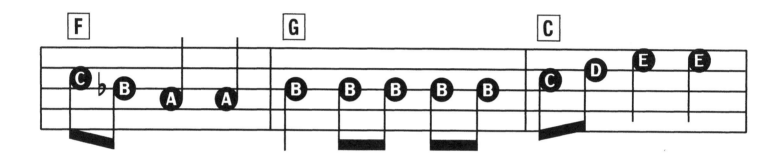

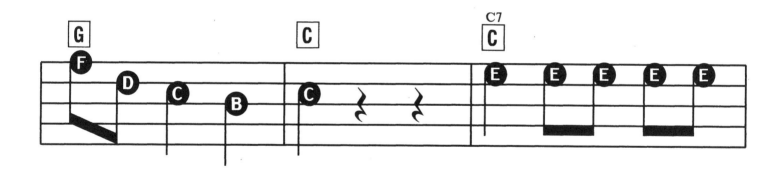

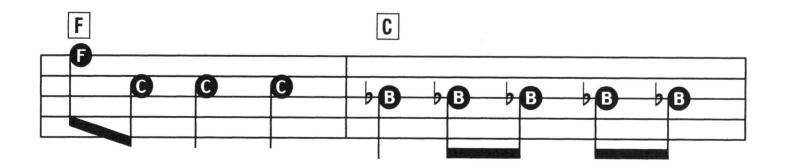

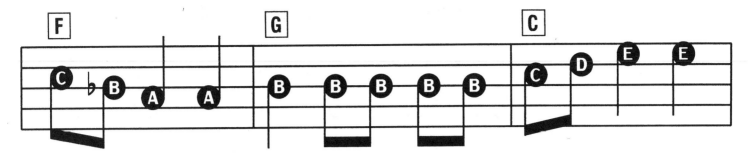

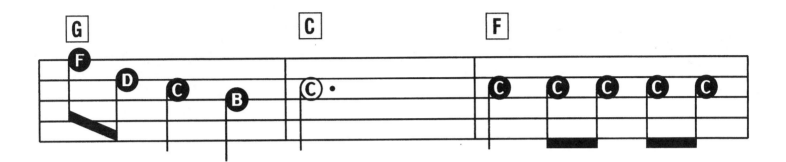

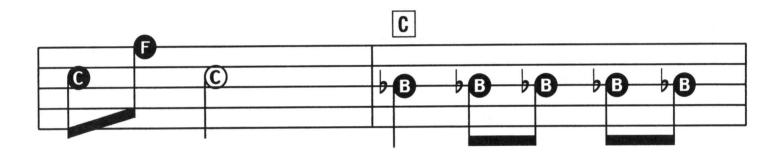

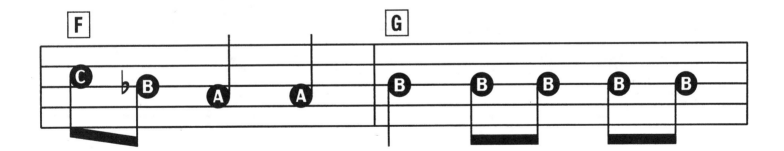

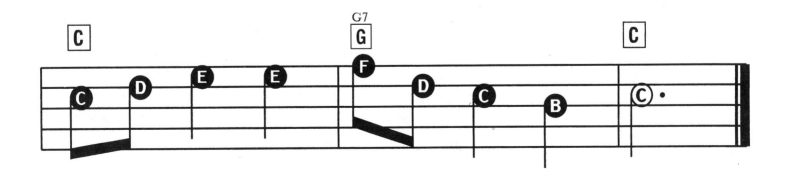

Minuet in F Major
K. 2

Registration 8
Rhythm: Waltz or None

By Wolfgang Amadeus Mozart

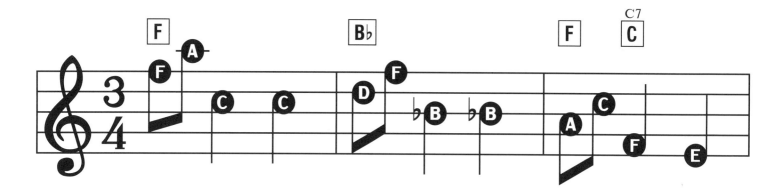

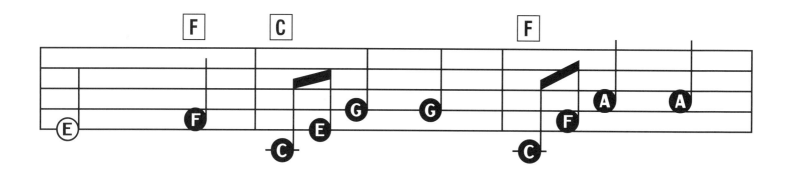

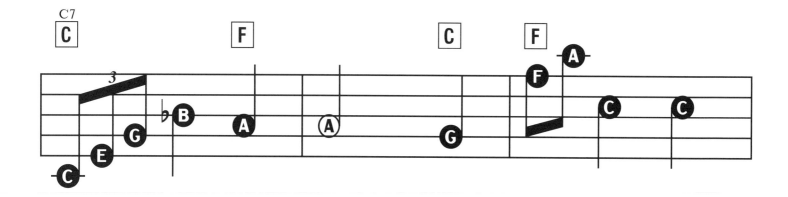

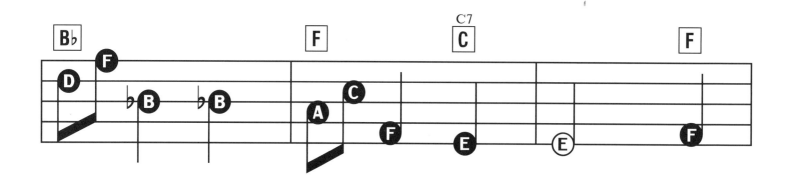

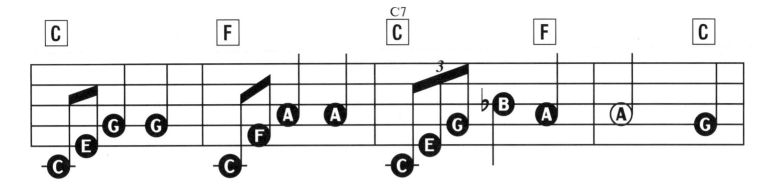

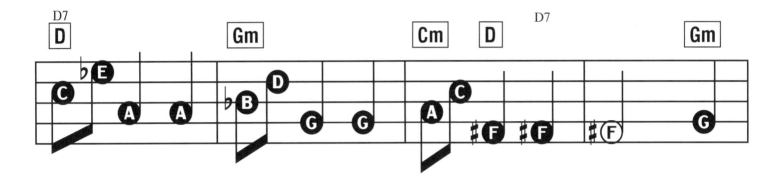

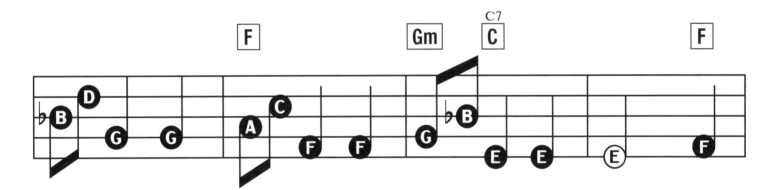

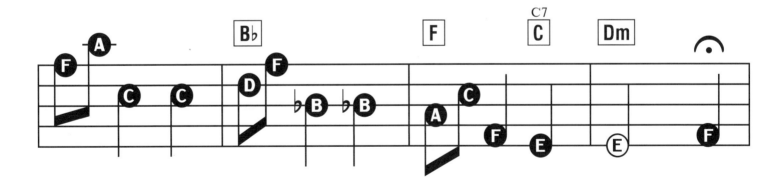

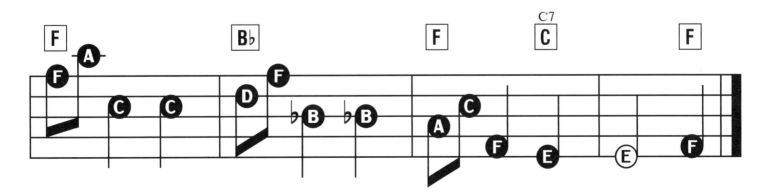

Non più andrai
from LE NOZZE DI FIGARO

Registration 4
Rhythm: Swing or Shuffle

By Wolfgang Amadeus Mozart

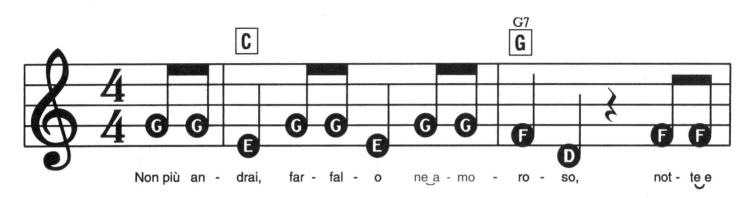

Non più an - drai, far - fal - o ne a - mo - ro - so, not - te e

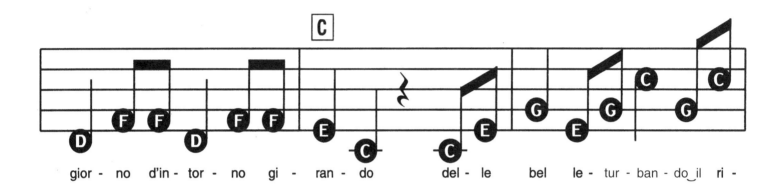

gior - no d'in - tor - no gi - ran - do del - le bel le - tur - ban - do il ri -

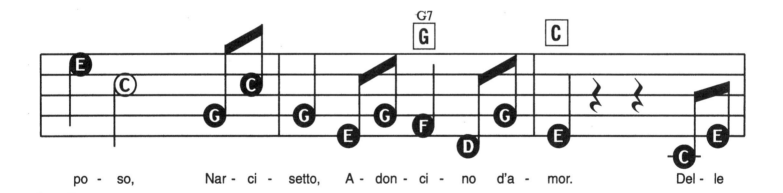

po - so, Nar - ci - setto, A - don - ci - no d'a - mor. Del - le

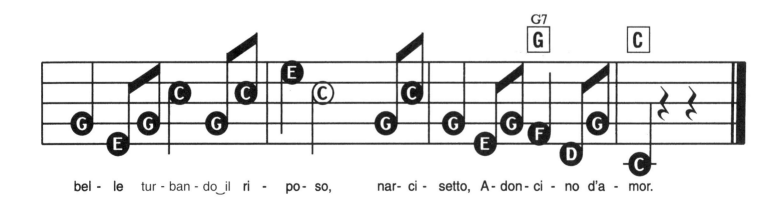

bel - le tur - ban - do il ri - po - so, nar - ci - setto, A - don - ci - no d'a - mor.

Piano Concerto No. 21 in C Major
("Elvira Madigan")
Second Movement

Registration 8
Rhythm: Ballad

By Wolfgang Amadeus Mozart

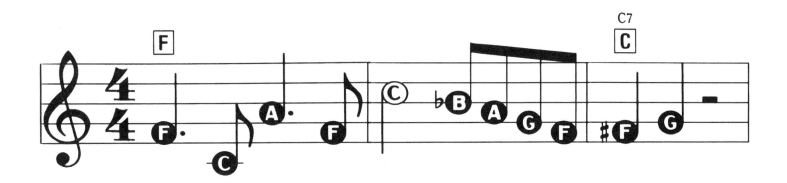

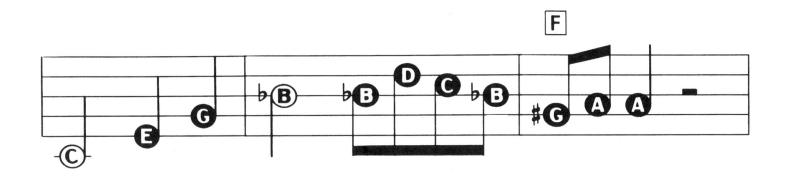

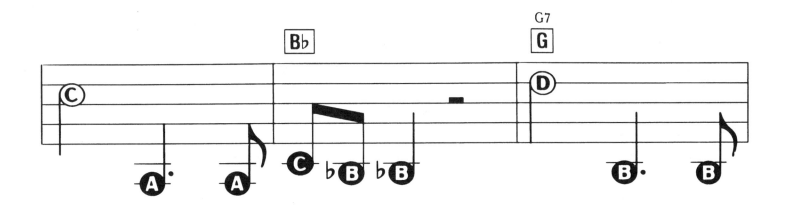

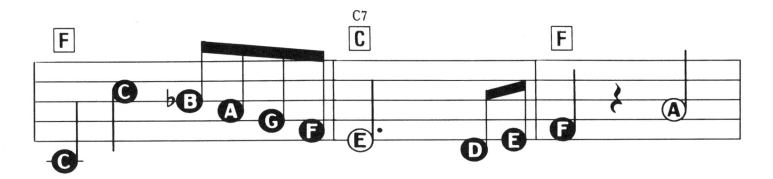

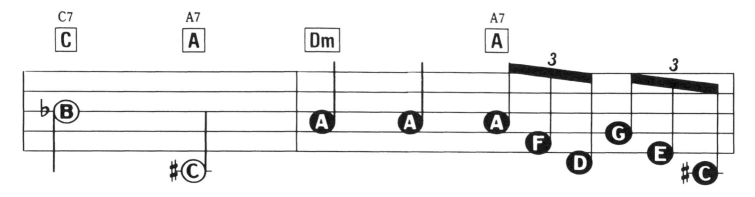

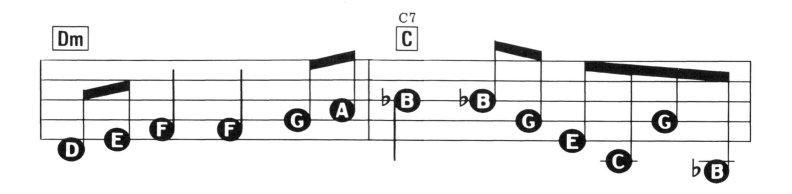

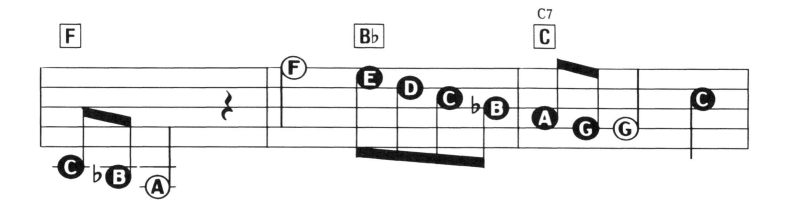

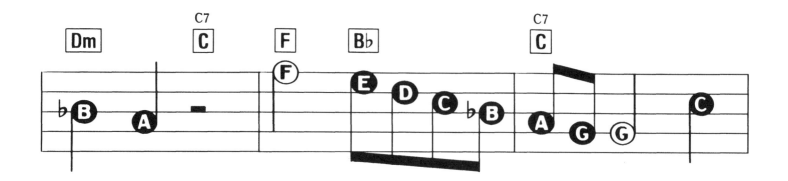

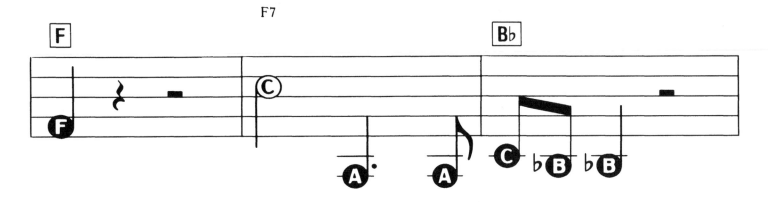

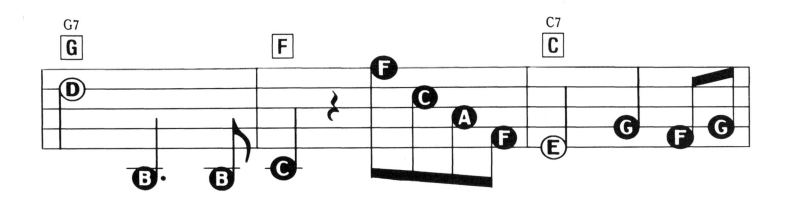

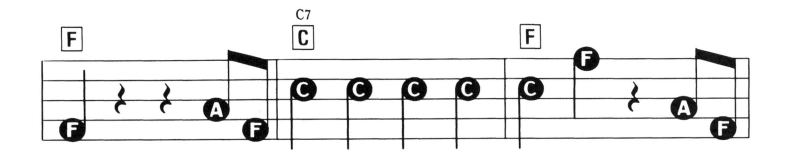

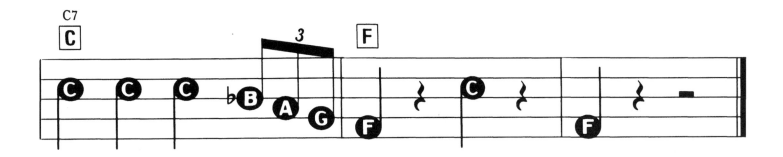

Symphony No. 40 in G Minor
First Movement (Molto allegro)

Registration 3
Rhythm: Fox Trot or None

By Wolfgang Amadeus Mozart

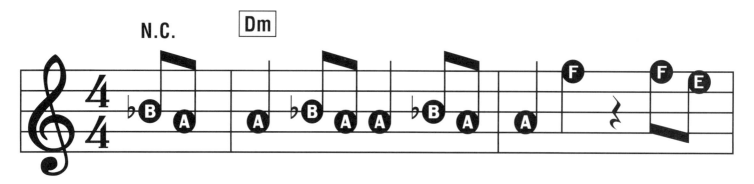

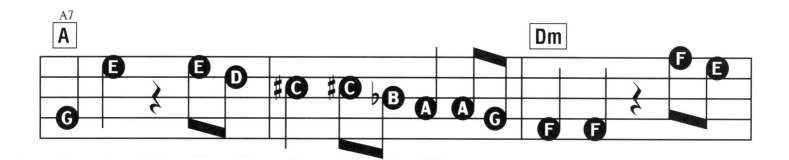

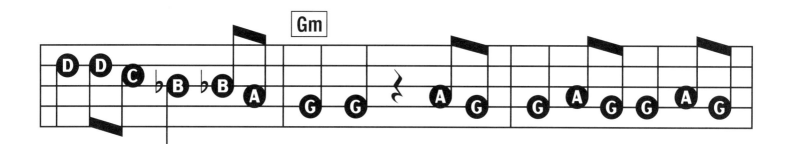

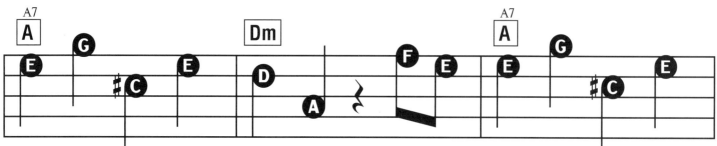

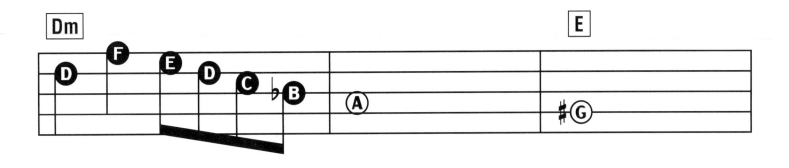

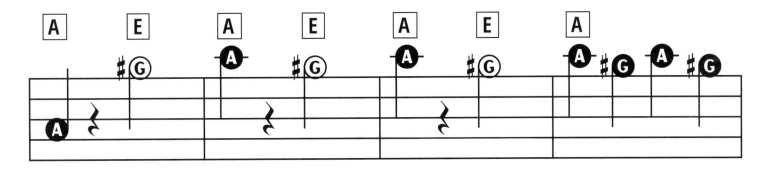

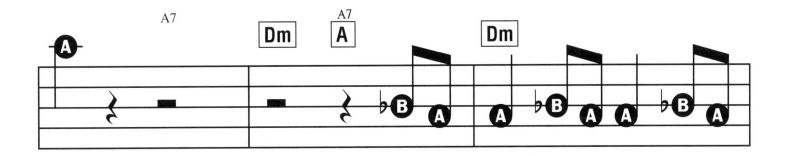

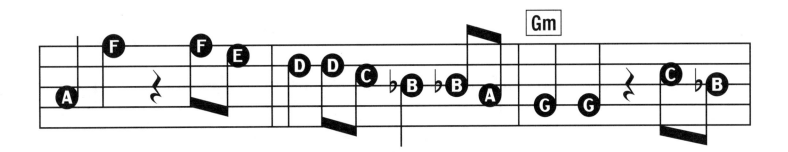

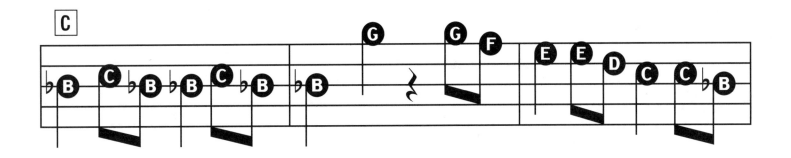

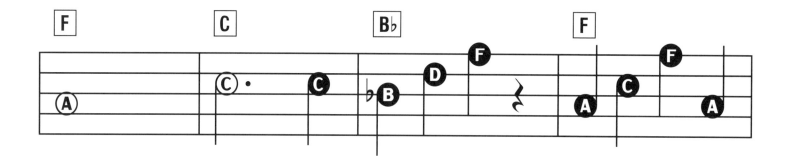

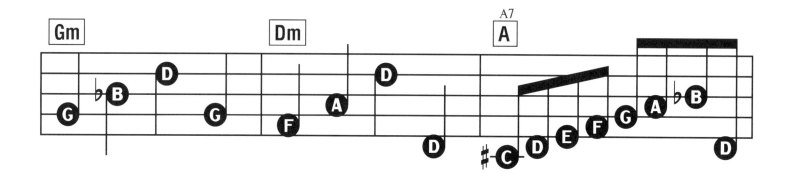

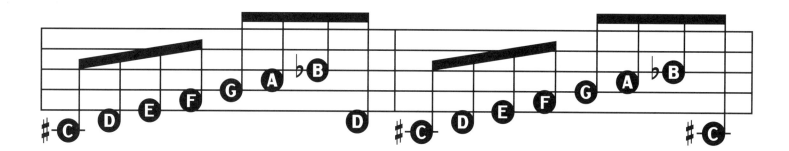

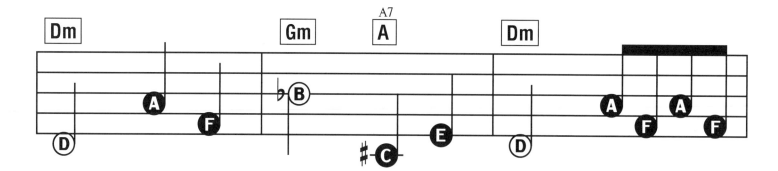

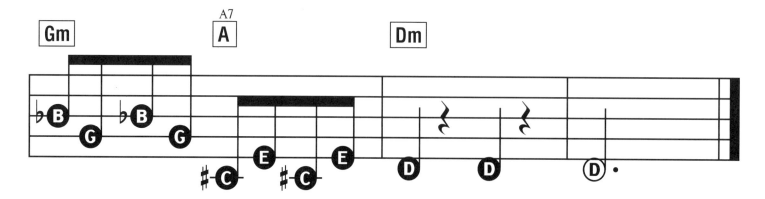

Symphony No. 40 in G Minor
Third Movement (Minuet)

Registration 3
Rhythm: Waltz or None

By Wolfgang Amadeus Mozart

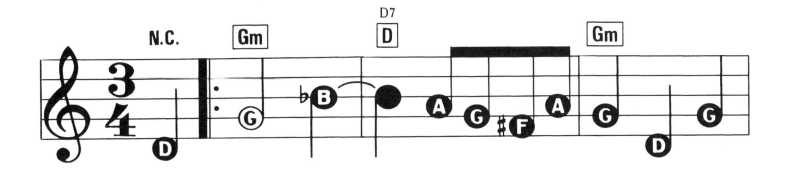

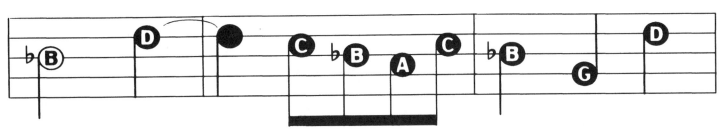

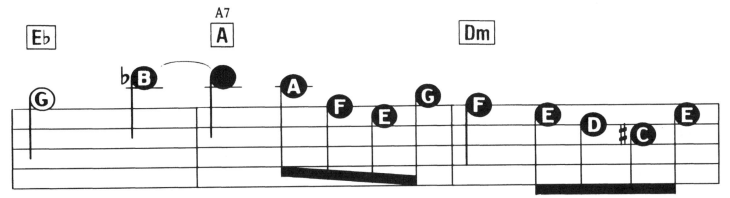

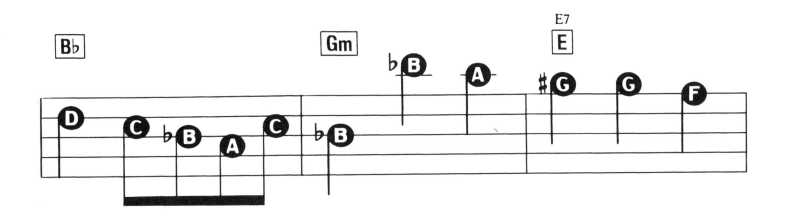

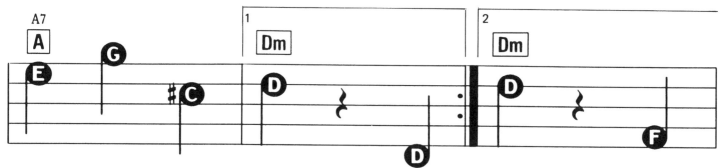

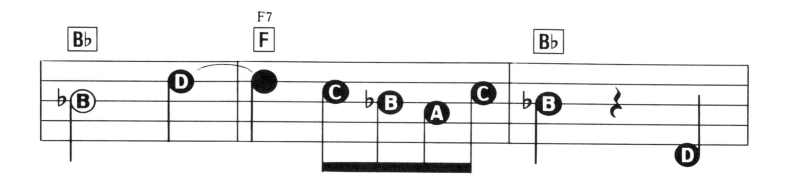

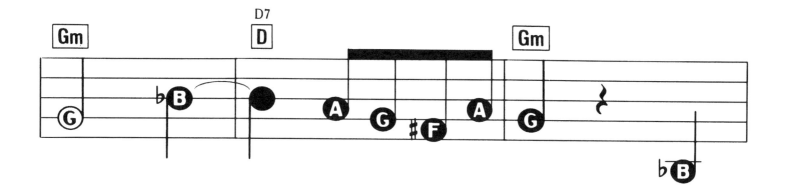

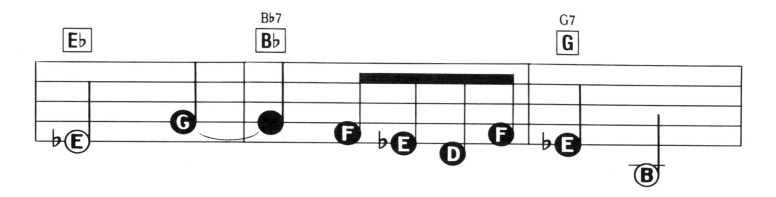

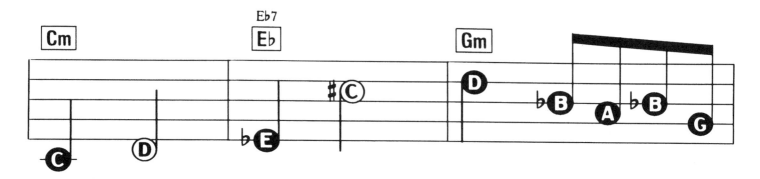

53

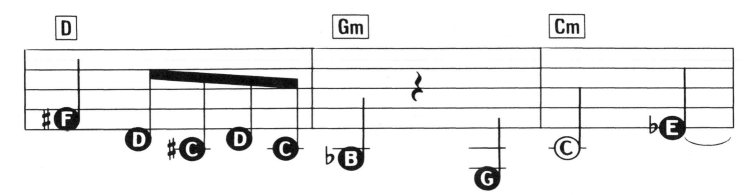

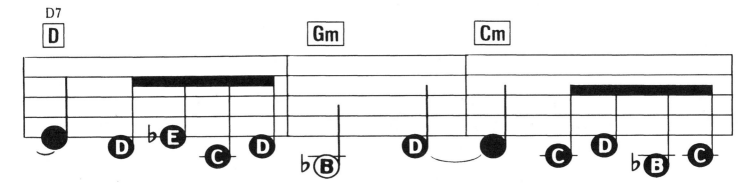

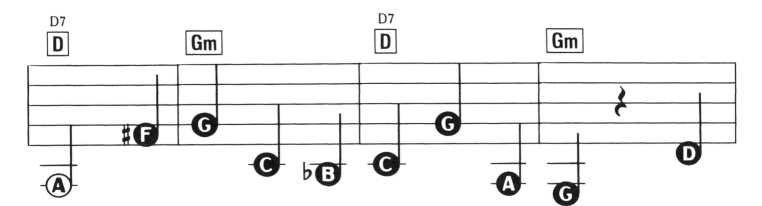

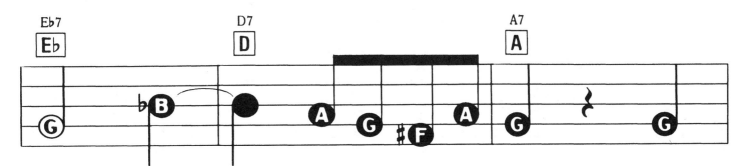

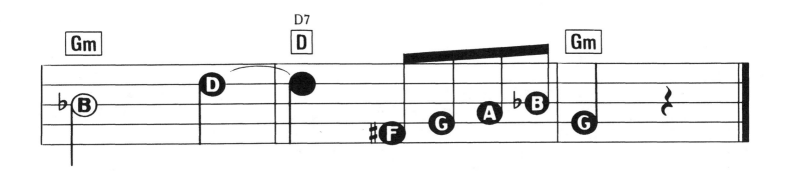

Turkish Rondo
from SONATA IN A MAJOR, K. 331

Registration 8
Rhythm: Latin or Rhumba

By Wolfgang Amadeus Mozart

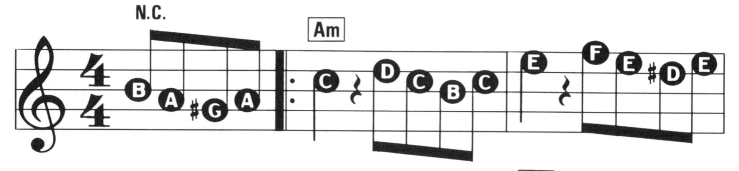

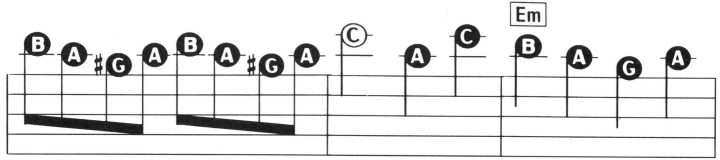

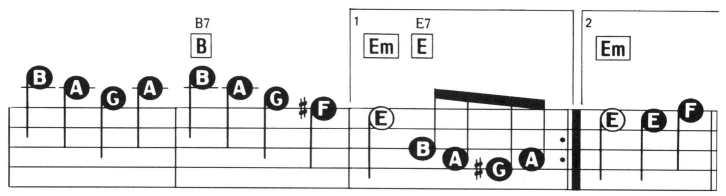

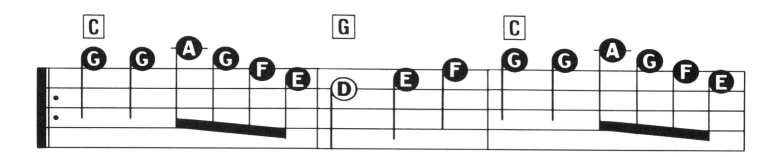

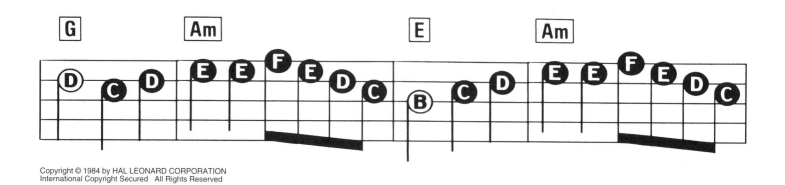

55

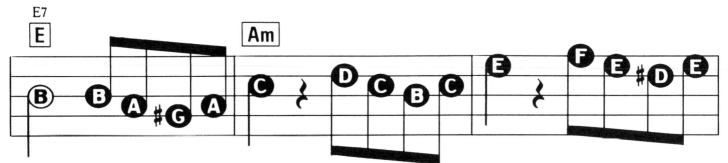

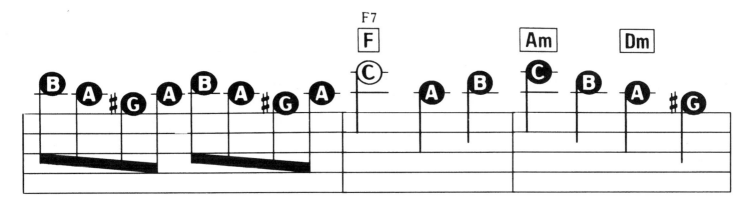

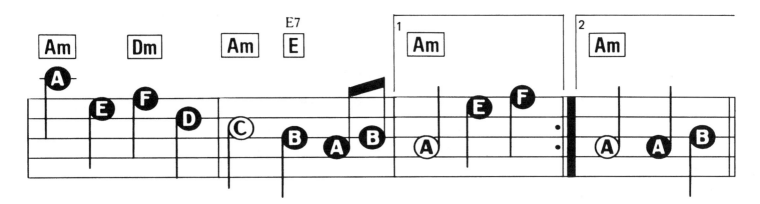

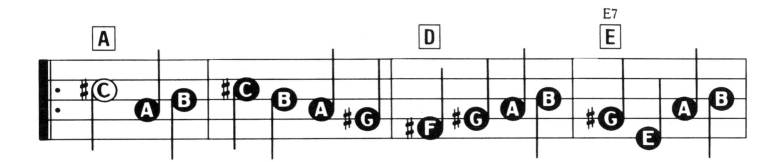

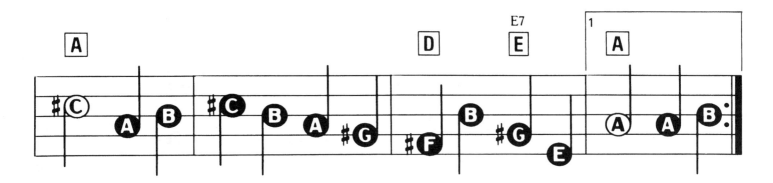

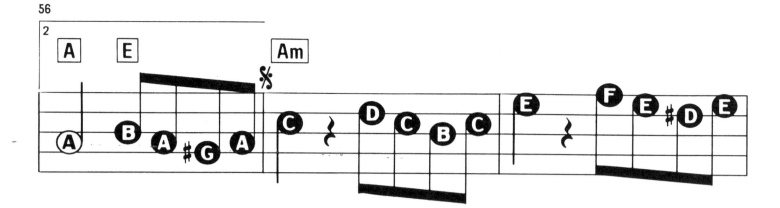

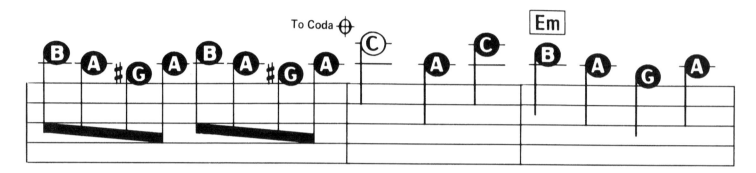

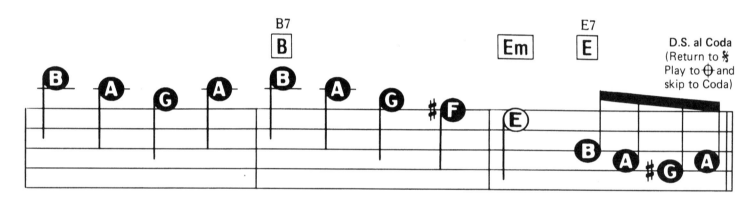

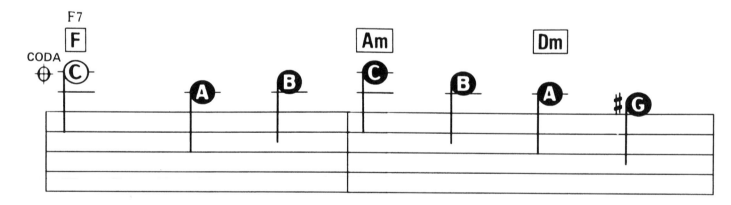

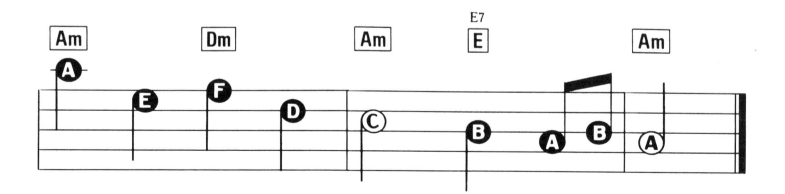